The Prince

NICCOLÒ MACHIAVELLI

Translated by
LUIGI RICCI

CONTENTS

MACHIAVELLI'S DEDICATION
TO LORENZO THE MAGNIFICENT
LORENZO THE MAGNIFICENT

It is customary for those who wish to gain the favour of a prince to endeavour to do so by offering him gifts of those things which they hold most precious, or in which they know him to take especial delight. In this way princes are often presented with horses, arms, cloth of gold, gems, and such-like ornaments worthy of their grandeur. In my desire, however, to offer to Your Highness some humble testimony of my devotion, I have been unable to find among my possessions anything which I hold so dear or esteem so highly as that knowledge of the deeds of great men which I have acquired through a long experience of modern events and a constant study of the past.

The results of my long observations and reflections are recorded in the little volume which I now offer to Your Highness: and although I deem this work unworthy of Your Highness's notice, yet my confidence in your humanity assures me that you will accept it, knowing that it is not in my power to offer you a greater gift than that of enabling you to understand in the shortest possible time all those things which I have learnt through danger and suffering in the course of many years. I have not sought to adorn my work with long phrases or high-sounding words or any of those allurements and ornaments with which many writers seek to embellish their books, as I desire no honour for my work but such as its truth and the gravity of its subject may justly deserve. Nor will it, I trust, be deemed presumptuous on the part of a man of humble and obscure condition to attempt to discuss and criticise the government of princes; for in the same way that landscape painters station themselves in the valleys in order to draw mountains or elevated ground, and ascend an eminence in order to get a good view of the plains, so it is necessary to be a prince to be able to know thoroughly the nature of a people, and to know the nature of princes one must be one of the populace.

May I trust, therefore, that Your Highness will accept this little gift in the spirit in which it is offered; and if Your Highness will deign to peruse it, you will recognise in it my ardent desire that you may attain to that grandeur which fortune and your own merits presage for you.

And should Your Highness gaze down from the summit of that eminence towards this humble spot, you will recognise the great and unmerited sufferings inflicted on me by a cruel fate.

THE PRINCE

I. THE VARIOUS KINDS OF GOVERNMENT AND THE WAYS BY WHICH THEY ARE ESTABLISHED

All states and dominions which hold or have held sway over mankind are either republics or monarchies. Monarchies are either hereditary ones, in which the rulers have been for many years of the same family, or else they are those of recent foundation. The newly founded ones are either entirely new, as was Milan to Francesco Sforza, or else they are, as it were, new members grafted on to the hereditary possessions of the prince that annexes them, as is the kingdom of Naples to the King of Spain. The dominions thus acquired have either been previously accustomed to the rule of another prince, or else have been free states, and they are annexed either by force of arms of the prince, or of others, or else fall to him by good fortune or merit.

II. OF HEREDITARY MONARCHIES

I will not here speak of republics, having already treated of them fully in another place. I will deal only with monarchies, and will show how the various kinds described above can be governed and maintained. In the first place, in hereditary states accustomed to the reigning family the difficulty of maintaining them is far less than in new monarchies; for it is sufficient not to exceed the ancestral usages, and to accommodate one's self to accidental circumstances; in this way such a prince, if of ordinary ability, will always be able to maintain his position, unless some very exceptional and excessive force deprives him of it; and even if he be thus deprived of it, on the slightest misfortune happening to the new occupier, he will be able to regain it.

We have in Italy the example of the Duke of Ferrara, who was able to withstand the assaults of the Venetians in the year '84, and of Pope Julius in the year '10, for no other reason than because of the antiquity of his family in that dominion. In as much as the legitimate prince has less cause and less necessity to give offence, it is only natural that he should be more loved; and, if no extraordinary vices make him hated, it is only reasonable for his subjects to be naturally attached to him, the memories and causes of innovations being forgotten in the long period over which his rule has existed; whereas one change always leaves the way prepared for the introduction of another.

III. OF MIXED MONARCHIES

But it is in the new monarchy that difficulties really exist. Firstly, if it is not entirely new, but a member as it were of a mixed state, its disorders spring at first from a natural difficulty which exists in all new dominions, because men change masters willingly, hoping to better themselves; and this belief makes them take arms against their rulers, in which they are deceived, as experience shows them that they have gone from bad to worse. This is the result of another very natural cause, which is the necessary harm inflicted on those over whom the prince obtains dominion, both by his soldiers and by an infinite number of other injuries unavoidably caused by his occupation.

Thus you find enemies in all those whom you have injured by occupying that dominion, and you cannot maintain the friendship of those who have helped you to obtain this possession, as you will not be able to fulfil their expectations, nor can you use strong measures with them, being under an obligation to them; for which reason, however strong your armies may be, you will always need the favour of the inhabitants to take possession of a province. It was from these causes that Louis XII. of France, though able to occupy Milan without trouble, immediately lost it, and the forces of Ludovico alone were sufficient to take it from him the first time, for the inhabitants who had willingly opened their gates to him, finding themselves deluded in the hopes they had cherished and not obtaining those benefits that they had anticipated, could not bear the vexatious rule of their new prince.

It is indeed true that, after reconquering the rebel territories they are not so easily lost again, for the ruler is now, by the fact of the rebellion, less averse to secure his position by punishing offenders, investigating any suspicious circumstances, and strengthening himself in weak places. So that although the mere appearance of such a person as Duke Ludovico on the frontier was sufficient to cause France to lose Milan the first time, to make her lose her grip of it the second time was only possible when all the world was against her, and after her enemies had been defeated and driven out of Italy; which was the result of the causes above mentioned. Nevertheless it was taken from her both the first and the second time. The general causes of the first loss have been already discussed; it remains now to be seen what were the causes of the second loss and by what means France could have avoided it, or what measures might have been taken by another ruler in that position which were not taken by the King of France. Be it observed, therefore, that those states which on annexation are united to a previously existing state may or may not be of the same nationality and language. If they are, it is very easy to hold them, especially if they are not accustomed to freedom; and to possess them securely it suffices that the family of the princes which formerly governed them be extinct. For the rest, their old condition not being disturbed, and there being no dissimilarity of customs, the people settle down quietly under their new rulers, as is seen in the case of Burgundy, Brittany, Gascony, and Normandy, which have been so long united to France; and although there may be some slight differences of language, the customs of the people are nevertheless similar, and they can get along well together, and whoever obtains possession of them and wishes to retain them must bear in mind two things: the one, that the blood of their old rulers is extinct; the other, to make no alteration either in their laws or in their taxes; in this way they will in a very short space of time become united with their old possessions and form one state. But when dominions are acquired in a province differing in language, laws, and customs, the difficulties to be overcome are great, and it requires good fortune as well as great industry to retain them; one of the best and most certain means of doing so would be for the new ruler to take up his residence in them. This would render their possession more secure and durable, it is what the Turk has done in Greece; in spite of all the other measures taken by him to hold that state, it would not have been possible to retain it had he not gone to live there. Being on the spot, disorders can be seen as they arise and can quickly be remedied, but living at a distance, they are only heard of when they get beyond remedy. Besides which, the province is not despoiled by your officials, the subjects are pleased with the easy accessibility of their prince; and wishing to be loyal they have more reason to love him, and should they be otherwise they will have greater cause to fear him.

Any external Power who wishes to assail that state will be less disposed to do so; so that as long as he resides there he will be very hard to dispossess. The other and better remedy is to plant colonies in one or two of those places which form as it were the keys of the land, for it is necessary either to do this or to maintain a large force of armed men. The colonies will cost the prince little; with little or no expense on his part, he can send and maintain them; he only injures those whose lands and houses are taken to give to the new inhabitants, and these form but a small proportion of the state, and those who are injured, remaining poor and scattered, can never do any harm to him, and all the others are, on the one hand, not injured and therefore easily pacified; and, on the other, are fearful of offending lest they should be treated like those who have been dispossessed of their property. To conclude, these colonies cost nothing, are more faithful, and give less offence; and the injured parties being poor and scattered are unable to do mischief, as I have shown. For it must be noted, that men must either be caressed or else annihilated; they will revenge themselves for small injuries, but cannot do so for great ones; the injury therefore that we do to a man must be such that we need not fear his vengeance. But by maintaining a garrison instead of colonists, one will spend much more, and consume in guarding it all the revenues of that state, so that the acquisition will result in a loss, besides giving much greater offence, since it injures every one in that state with the quartering of the army on it; which being an inconvenience felt** by all, every one becomes an enemy, and these are enemies which can do mischief, as, though beaten, they remain in their own homes. In every way, therefore, a garrison is as useless as colonies are useful. Further, the ruler of a foreign province as described, should make himself the leader and defender of his less powerful neighbours, and endeavour to weaken the stronger ones, and take care that his possessions are not entered by some foreigner not less powerful than himself, who will always intervene at the request of those who are discontented either through ambition or fear, as was seen when the Ætoli invited the Romans into Greece; and in whatever province they entered, it was always at the request of the inhabitants. And the rule is that when a powerful foreigner enters a province, all the less powerful inhabitants become his adherents, moved by the envy they bear to those ruling over them; so much so that with regard to these minor potentates he has no trouble whatever in winning them over, for they willingly join forces with the state that he has acquired. He has merely to be careful that they do not assume too much power and authority, and he can easily with his own forces and their favour put down those that are powerful and remain in everything the arbiter of that province. And he who does not govern well in this way will soon lose what he has acquired, and while he holds it will meet with infinite difficulty and trouble.

The Romans in the provinces they took, always followed this policy; they established colonies, flattered the less powerful without increasing their strength, put down the most powerful and did not allow foreign rulers to obtain influence in them. I will let the single province of Greece suffice as an example. They made friends with the Achæi and the Ætoli, the kingdom of Macedonia was cast down, and Antiochus driven out, nor did they allow the merits of the Achæi or the Ætoli to gain them any increase of territory, nor did the persuasions of Philip induce them to befriend him without lowering him, nor could the power of Antiochus make them consent to allow him to hold any state in that province.

For the Romans did in this case what all wise princes should do, who look not only at present dangers but also at future ones and diligently guard against them; for being foreseen they can easily be remedied, but if one waits till they are at hand, the medicine is no longer in time as the malady has become incurable; it happening with this as with those hectic fevers spoken of by doctors, which at their beginning are easy to cure but difficult to recognise, but in course of time when they have not at first been recognised and treated, become easy to recognise and difficult to cure. Thus it happens in matters of state; for knowing afar off (which it is only given to a prudent man to do) the evils that are brewing, they are easily cured. But when, for want of such knowledge, they are allowed to grow so that every one can recognise them, there is no longer any remedy to be found. However, the Romans, observing these disorders while yet remote, were always able to find a remedy, and never allowed them to proceed in order to avoid a war; for they knew that war was not to be avoided, and could be deferred only to the advantage of the other side; they therefore declared war against Philip and Antiochus in Greece, so as not to have to fight them in Italy, though they might at the time have avoided either; this they did not choose to do, never caring to do that which is now every day to be heard in the mouths of our wise men, to enjoy the benefits of time, but preferring those of their own virtue and prudence, for time brings with it all things, and may produce indifferently either good or evil. But let us return to

France and examine whether she did any of these things; and I will speak not of Charles, but of Louis as the one whose proceedings can be better seen, as he held possession in Italy for a longer time; you will then see that he did the opposite of all those things which must be done to keep possession of a foreign state. King Louis was called into Italy by the ambition of the Venetians, who wished by his coming to gain half of Lombardy. I will not blame the king for coming nor for the part he took, because wishing to plant his foot in Italy, and not having friends in the country, on the contrary the conduct of King Charles having caused all doors to be closed to him, he was forced to accept what friendships he could find, and his schemes would have quickly been successful if he had made no mistakes in his other proceedings.

The king then having acquired Lombardy regained immediately the reputation lost by Charles. Genoa yielded, the Florentines became his friends, the Marquis of Mantua, the Dukes of Ferrara and Bentivogli, the Lady of Furlì, the Lords of Faenza, Pesaro, Rimini, Camerino, and Piombino, the inhabitants of Lucca, of Pisa, and of Sienna, all approached him with offers of friendship. The Venetians might then have seen the effects of their temerity, how to gain a few lands in Lombardy they had made the king ruler over two-thirds of Italy. Consider how little difficulty the king would have had in maintaining his reputation in Italy if he had observed the rules above given, and kept a firm and sure hold over all those friends of his, who being many in number, and weak, and fearful one of the Church, another of the Venetians, were always obliged to hold fast to him, and by whose aid he could easily make sure of any who were still great. But he was hardly in Milan before he did exactly the opposite, by giving aid to Pope Alexander to occupy the Romagna. Nor did he perceive that, in taking this course, he weakened himself, by casting off his friends and those who had placed themselves at his disposal, and strengthened the Church by adding to the spiritual power, which gives it such authority, further temporal powers. And having made the first mistake, he was obliged to follow it up, whilst, to put a stop to the ambition of Alexander and prevent him becoming ruler of Tuscany, he was forced to come to Italy. And not content with having increased the power of the Church and lost his friends, he now desiring the kingdom of Naples, divided it with the king of Spain; and where he alone was the arbiter of Italy, he now brought in a companion, so that the ambitious of that province who were dissatisfied with him might have some one else to appeal to; and where he might have left in that kingdom a king tributary to him, he dispossessed him in order to bring in another who was capable of driving him out. The desire to acquire possessions is a very natural and ordinary thing, and when those men do it who can do so successfully, they are always praised and not blamed, but when they cannot and yet want to do so at all costs, they make a mistake deserving of great blame. If France, therefore, with her own forces could have taken Naples, she ought to have done so; if she could not she ought not to have divided it. And if the partition of Lombardy with the Venetians is to be excused, as having been the means of allowing the French king to set foot in Italy, this other partition deserves blame, not having the excuse of necessity.

Louis had thus made these five mistakes: he had crushed the smaller Powers, increased the power in Italy of one ruler, brought into the land a very powerful foreigner, and he had not come to live there himself, nor had he established any colonies. Still these mistakes might, if he had lived, not have injured him, had he not made the sixth, that of taking the state from the Venetians; for, if he had not strengthened the Church and brought the Spaniards into Italy, it would have been right and necessary to humble them; having once taken those measures, he ought never to have consented to their ruin; because, had the Venetians been strong, it would have kept the others from making attempts on Lombardy, partly because the Venetians would not have consented to any measures by which they did not get it for themselves, and partly because the others would not have wanted to take it from France to give it to Venice, and would not have had the courage to attack both.

If any one urges that King Louis yielded the Romagna to Alexander and the kingdom to Spain in order to avoid war, I reply, with the reasons already given, that one ought never to allow a disorder to take place in order to avoid war, for war is not thereby avoided, but only deferred to your disadvantage. And if others allege the promise given by the king to the pope to undertake that enterprise for him, in return for the dissolution of his marriage and for the cardinalship of Rohan, I reply with what I shall say later on about the faith of princes and how it is to be observed. Thus King Louis lost Lombardy through not observing any of those conditions which have been observed by others who have taken provinces and wished to retain them. Nor is this any miracle, but very reasonable and natural. I spoke of this matter with Cardinal Rohan at Nantes when Valentine, as Cesare Borgia, son of Pope Alexander, was commonly called, was occupying the Romagna, for on Cardinal Rohan saying to me that the Italians did not understand war, I replied that the French did not understand politics, for if they did they would never allow the Church to become so great. And experience shows us that the greatness in Italy of the Church and also of Spain have been caused by France, and her ruin has proceeded from them. From which may be drawn a general rule, which never or very rarely fails, that whoever is the cause of another becoming powerful, is ruined himself; for that power is produced by him either through craft or force; and both of these are suspected by the one that has become powerful.

IV. WHY THE KINGDOM OF DARIUS, OCCUPIED BY ALEXANDER, DID NOT REBEL AGAINST THE SUCCESSORS OF THE LATTER AFTER HIS DEATH.

Considering the difficulties there are in holding a newly acquired state, some may wonder how it came to pass that Alexander the Great became master of Asia in a few years, and had hardly occupied it when he died, from which it might be supposed that the whole state would have rebelled. However, his successors maintained themselves in possession, and had no further difficulty in doing so than those which arose among themselves from their own ambitions.

I reply that the kingdoms known to history have been governed in two ways: either by a prince and his servants, who, as ministers by his grace and permission, assist in governing the realm; or by a prince and by barons, who hold their positions not by favour of the ruler but by antiquity of blood. Such barons have states and subjects of their own, who recognise them as their lords, and are naturally attached to them. In those states which are governed by a prince and his servants, the prince possesses more authority, because there is no one in the state regarded as a superior besides himself, and if others are obeyed it is merely as ministers and officials of the prince, and no one regards them with any special affection. Examples of these two kinds of government in our own time are the Turk and the King of France. All the Turkish monarchy is governed by one ruler, the others are his servants, and dividing his kingdom into "sangiacates," he sends to them various administrators, and changes or recalls them at his pleasure. But the King of France is surrounded by a large number of ancient nobles, recognised as such by their subjects, and loved by them; they have their prerogatives, which the king cannot deprive them of without danger to himself. Whoever now considers these two states will see that it would be difficult to acquire the state of the Turk; but having conquered it, it would be very easy to hold it.

The causes of the difficulty of occupying the Turkish kingdom are, that the invader could not be invited by princes of that kingdom, nor hope to facilitate his enterprise by the rebellion of those around him, as will be evident from reasons given above. Because, being all slaves, and bound, it will be more difficult to corrupt them, and even if they were corrupted, little effect could be hoped for, as they would not be able to carry the people with them for the reasons mentioned. Therefore, whoever assaults the Turk must be prepared to meet his united forces, and must rely more on his own strength than on the disorders of others; but having once conquered him, and beaten him in battle so that he can no longer raise armies, nothing else is to be feared except the family of the prince, and if this is extinguished, there is no longer any one to be feared, the others having no credit with the people; and as the victor before the victory could place no hope in them, so he need not fear them afterwards. The contrary is the case in kingdoms governed like that of France, because it is easy to enter them by winning over some baron of the kingdom, there being always some malcontents, and those desiring innovations. These can, for the reasons stated, open the way to you and facilitate victory; but afterwards, if you wish to keep possession, infinite difficulties arise, both from those who have aided you and from those you have oppressed. Nor is it sufficient to extinguish the family of the prince, for there remain those nobles who will make themselves the head of new changes, and being neither able to content them nor exterminate them, you will lose the state whenever an occasion arises. Now if you will consider what was the nature of the government of Darius you will find it similar to the kingdom of the Turk, and therefore Alexander had first to completely overthrow it and seize the country, after which victory, Darius being dead, the state remained secure to Alexander, for the reasons discussed above. And his successors, had they remained united, might have enjoyed it in peace, nor did any tumults arise in the kingdom except those fomented by themselves. But it is impossible to possess with such ease countries constituted like France.

Hence arose the frequent rebellions of Spain, France, and Greece against the Romans, owing to the numerous principalities which existed in those states; for, as long as the memory of these lasted, the Romans were always uncertain of their possessions; but when the memory of these principalities had been extinguished they became, with the power and duration of the empire, secure possessions.

And afterwards the latter could, when fighting among themselves, draw each one with him a portion of these provinces, according to the authority he had established there, and these provinces, when the family of their ancient princes was extinct, recognised no other rulers but the Romans. Considering these things, therefore, let no one be surprised at the facility with which Alexander could hold Asia, and at the difficulties that others have had in holding acquired possessions, like Pyrrhus and many others; as this was not caused by the greater or smaller ability of the conqueror, but depended on the dissimilarity of the conditions.

V. THE WAY TO GOVERN CITIES OR DOMINIONS THAT, PREVIOUS TO BEING OCCUPIED, LIVED UNDER THEIR OWN LAWS

When those states which have been acquired are accustomed to live at liberty under their own laws, there are three ways of holding them. The first is to ruin them; the second is to go and live there in person; the third is to allow them to live under their own laws, taking tribute of them, and creating there within the country a state composed of a few who will keep it friendly to you. Because this state, being created by the prince, knows that it cannot exist without his friendship and protection, and will do all it can to keep them, and a city used to liberty can be more easily held by means of its citizens than in any other way, if you wish to preserve it. There is the example of the Spartans and the Romans. The Spartans held Athens and Thebes by creating within them a state of a few people; nevertheless they lost them. The Romans, in order to hold Capua, Carthage, and Numantia, destroyed them, but did not lose them. They wanted to hold Greece in almost the same way as the Spartans held it, leaving it free and under its own laws, but they did not succeed; so that they were compelled to destroy many cities in that province in order to keep it, because in truth there is no sure method of holding them except by ruining them. And whoever becomes the ruler of a free city and does not destroy it, can expect to be destroyed by it, for it can always find a motive for rebellion in the name of liberty and of its ancient usages, which are forgotten neither by lapse of time nor by benefits received, and whatever one does or provides, so long as the inhabitants are not separated or dispersed, they do not forget that name and those usages, but appeal to them at once in every emergency, as did Pisa after being so many years held in servitude by the Florentines. But when cities or provinces have been accustomed to live under a prince, and the family of that prince is extinguished, being on the one hand used to obey, and on the other not having their old prince, they cannot unite in choosing one from among themselves, and they do not know how to live in freedom, so that they are slower to take arms, and a prince can win them over with greater facility and establish himself securely. But in republics there is greater life, greater hatred, and more desire for vengeance; they do not and cannot cast aside the memory of their ancient liberty, so that the surest way is either to destroy them or reside in them.

VI. OF NEW DOMINIONS WHICH HAVE BEEN ACQUIRED BY ONE'S OWN ARMS AND POWERS

Let no one marvel if in speaking of new dominions both as to prince and state, I bring forward very exalted instances, for as men walk almost always in the paths trodden by others, proceeding in their actions by imitation, and not being always able to follow others exactly, nor attain to the excellence of those they imitate, a prudent man should always follow in the path trodden by great men and imitate those who are most excellent, so that if he does not attain to their greatness, at any rate he will get some tinge of it. He will do like prudent archers, who when the place they wish to hit is too far off, knowing how far their bow will carry, aim at a spot much higher than the one they wish to hit, not in order to reach this height with their arrow, but by help of this high aim to hit the spot they wish to. I say then that in new dominions, where there is a new prince, it is more or less easy to hold them according to the greater or lesser ability of him who acquires them. And as the fact of a private individual becoming a prince presupposes either great ability or good fortune, it would appear that either of these things would mitigate in part many difficulties. Nevertheless those who have been wanting as regards good fortune have maintained themselves best. The matter is also facilitated by the prince being obliged to reside personally in his territory, having no others. But to come to those who have become princes through their own merits and not by fortune, I regard as the greatest, Moses, Cyrus, Romulus, Theseus, and such like. And although one should not speak of Moses, he having merely carried out what was ordered him by God, still he deserves admiration, if only for that grace which made him worthy to speak with God. But regarding Cyrus and others who have acquired or founded kingdoms, they will all be found worthy of admiration; and if their particular actions and methods are examined they will not appear very different from those of Moses, although he had so great a Master. And in examining their life and deeds it will be seen that they owed nothing to fortune but the opportunity which gave them matter to be shaped into the form that they thought fit; and without that opportunity their powers would have been wasted, and without their powers the opportunity would have come in vain. It was thus necessary that Moses should find the people of Israel slaves in Egypt and oppressed by the Egyptians, so that they were disposed to follow him in order to escape from their servitude. It was necessary that Romulus should be unable to remain in Alba, and should have been exposed at his birth, in order that he might become King of Rome and founder of that nation. It was necessary that Cyrus should find the Persians discontented with the empire of the Medes, and the Medes weak and effeminate through long peace. Theseus could not have showed his abilities if he had not found the Athenians dispersed.

These opportunities, therefore, gave these men their chance, and their own great qualities enabled them to profit by them, so as to ennoble their country and augment its fortunes. Those who by heroic means such as these become princes, obtain their dominions with difficulty but retain them easily, and the difficulties which they have in acquiring their dominions arise in part from the new rules and regulations that they have to introduce in order to establish their position securely. It must be considered that there is nothing more difficult to carry out, nor more doubtful of success, nor more dangerous to handle, than to initiate a new order of things. For the reformer has enemies in all those who profit by the old order, and only lukewarm defenders in all those who would profit by the new order, this lukewarmness arising partly from fear of their adversaries, who have the laws in their favour; and partly from the incredulity of mankind, who do not truly believe in anything new until they have had actual experience of it. Thus it arises that on every opportunity for attacking the reformer, his opponents do so with the zeal of partisans, the others only defend him half-heartedly, so that between them he runs great danger. It is necessary, however, in order to investigate thoroughly this question, to examine whether these innovators are independent, or whether they depend upon others, that is to say, whether in order to carry out their designs they have to entreat or are able to force. In the first case they invariably succeed ill, and accomplish nothing; but when they can depend on their own strength and are able to use force, they rarely fail. Thus it comes about that all armed prophets have conquered and unarmed ones failed; for besides what has been already said, the character of people varies, and it is easy to persuade them of a thing, but difficult to keep them in that persuasion. And so it is necessary to order things so that when they no longer believe, they can be made to believe by force. Moses, Cyrus, Theseus, and Romulus would not have been able to make their institutions observed for so long had they been disarmed, as happened in our own time to Fra Girolamo Savonarola, who failed entirely in his new rules when the multitude began to disbelieve in him, and he had no means of holding fast those who had believed nor of compelling the unbelievers to believe. Therefore such men as these have great difficulty in making their way, and all their dangers are met on the road and must be overcome by their own abilities; but when once they have overcome them and have begun to be held in veneration, and have suppressed those who envied them, they remain powerful and secure, honoured and happy. To the high examples given I will add a lesser one, which, however, is to be compared in some measure with them and will serve as an instance of all such cases, that of Hiero of Syracuse, who from a private individual became Prince of Siracusa, without other aid from fortune beyond the opportunity; for the

Siracusans being oppressed elected him as their captain, from which by merit he was made prince; while still in private life his virtues were such that it was written of him, that he lacked nothing to reign but the kingdom. He abolished the old militia, raised a new one, abandoned his old friendships and formed new ones; and as he had thus friends and soldiers of his own, he was able on this foundation to build securely, so that while he had great trouble in acquiring his position he had little in maintaining it.

VII. OF NEW DOMINIONS ACQUIRED BY THE POWER OF OTHERS OR BY FORTUNE

Those who rise from private citizens to be princes merely by fortune have little trouble in rising but very much in maintaining their position. They meet with no difficulties on the way as they fly over them, but all their difficulties arise when they are established. Such are they who are granted a state either for money, or by favour of him who grants it, as happened to many in Greece, in the cities of Ionia and of the Hellespont, who were created princes by Darius in order to hold these places for his security and glory; such were also those emperors who from private citizens became emperors by bribing the army. Such as these depend absolutely on the good will and fortune of those who have raised them, both of which are extremely inconstant and unstable. They neither know how to, nor are in a position to maintain their rank, for unless he be a man of great genius it is not likely that one who has always lived in a private position should know how to command, and they are unable to command because they possess no forces which will be friendly and faithful to them. Moreover, states quickly founded, like all other things which are born and grow rapidly, cannot have deep roots, so that the first storm destroys them, unless, as already said, the man who thus becomes a prince is of such great genius as to be able to take immediate steps for maintaining what fortune has thrown into his lap, and lay afterwards those foundations which others make before becoming princes. With regard to these two methods of becoming a prince,—by ability or by good fortune, I will here adduce two examples which have taken place within our memory, those of Francesco Sforza and Cesare Borgia.

Francesco, by appropriate means and through great abilities, from citizen became Duke of Milan, and what he had attained after a thousand difficulties he maintained with little trouble. On the other hand, Cesare Borgia, commonly called Duke Valentine, acquired the state through the fortune of his father and by the same means lost it, and that although every measure was adopted by him and everything done that a prudent and capable man could do to establish himself firmly in that state that the arms and the favours of others had given him. For, as we have said, he who does not lay his foundations beforehand may by great abilities do so afterwards, although with great trouble to the architect and danger to the building. If, then, one considers the progress made by the duke, it will be seen how firm were the foundations he had laid to his future power, which I do not think it superfluous to examine, as I know of no better precepts for a new prince to follow than the example of his actions; and if his measures were not successful, it was through no fault of his own but only by the most extraordinary malignity of fortune. In wishing to aggrandise the duke his son, Alexander VI. had to meet very great difficulties both present and future. In the first place, he saw no way of making him ruler of any state that was not a possession of the Church. And in attempting to take that of the Church, he knew that the Duke of Milan and the Venetians would not consent, because Faenza and Rimini were already under the protection of the Venetians. He saw, moreover, that the arms of Italy, especially of those who might have served him, were in the hands of those who would fear the greatness of the pope, and therefore he could not depend upon them, being all under the Orsinis and Colonnas and their adherents. It was, therefore, necessary to disturb the existing condition and bring about disorders in the states of Italy in order to obtain secure mastery over a part of them; this was easy, for he found the Venetians, who, actuated by other motives, had invited the French into Italy, which he not only did not oppose, but facilitated by dissolving the marriage of King Louis. The king came thus into Italy with the aid of the Venetians and the consent of Alexander, and had hardly arrived at Milan before the pope obtained troops from him for his enterprise in the Romagna, which he carried out by means of the reputation of the king. The duke having thus obtained the Romagna and defeated the Colonnas, was hindered in maintaining it and proceeding further by two things: the one, his forces, of which he doubted the fidelity; the other the will of France, that is to say, he feared lest the arms of the Orsini of which he had availed himself should fail him, and not only hinder him in obtaining more but take from him what he had already conquered, and he also feared that the king might do the same. He had evidence of this as regards the Orsini when, after taking Faenza, he assaulted Bologna and observed their backwardness in the assault. And as regards the king, he perceived his designs when, after taking the dukedom of Urbino, he attacked Tuscany, and the king made him desist from that enterprise; whereupon the duke decided to depend no longer on the fortunes and arms of others. The first thing he did was to weaken the parties of the Orsinis and Colonnas in Rome by gaining all their adherents who were gentlemen and making them followers of himself, by granting them large pensions, and appointing them to commands and offices according to their rank, so that their attachment to their parties was extinguished in a few months, and entirely concentrated on the duke. After this he awaited an opportunity for crushing the Orsinis, having dispersed the adherents of the Colonna family, and when the opportunity arrived he made good use of it, for the Orsini seeing at length that the greatness of the duke and of the Church meant their own ruin, convoked a diet at Magione in the Perugino. Hence sprang the rebellion of Urbino and the tumults in Romagna and infinite dangers to the duke, who overcame them all with the help of the French; and having regained his reputation, neither trusting France nor other foreign forces in order not to have to oppose them, he had recourse to stratagem. He dissembled his aims so well that the Orsini, through the mediation of Signor Pavolo, made their peace with him, which the duke spared no efforts to make secure, presenting them with robes, money, and horses, so that in their simplicity they were induced to come to Sinigaglia and fell into his hands. Having thus suppressed these leaders and made their partisans his friends, the duke had laid a very good foundation to his power, having all the Romagna with the duchy of Urbino, and having gained the favour of the inhabitants, who began to feel the benefit of his rule. And as this part is worthy of note and of imitation by others, I will not omit mention of it. When he took the Romagna, it had previously been governed by weak rulers, who had rather despoiled their subjects than governed them, and given them more cause for disunion than for union, so that the province was a prey to robbery, assaults, and every kind of disorder. He, therefore, judged it necessary to give them a good government in order to make them peaceful and obedient to his rule. For this purpose he appointed Messer Remiro d' Orco, a cruel and able man, to whom he gave the fullest authority. This man, in a short time, was highly successful in rendering the country orderly and united, whereupon the duke, not deeming such excessive authority expedient, lest it should become hateful, appointed a civil court of justice in the middle of the province under an excellent president, to which each city appointed its own advocate. And as he knew that the harshness of the past had engendered some amount of hatred, in order to purge the minds of the people and to win them over completely, he resolved to show that if any cruelty had taken place it was not by his orders, but through the harsh disposition of his minister. And taking him on some pretext, he had him placed one morning in the public square at Cesena, cut in half, with a piece of wood and blood-stained knife by his side. The ferocity of this spectacle caused the people both satisfaction and amazement. But to return to where we left off.

The duke being now powerful and partly secured against present perils, being armed himself, and having in a great measure put down those neighbouring forces which might injure him, had now to get the respect of France, if he wished to proceed with his acquisitions, for he knew that the king, who had lately discovered his error, would not give him any help. He began therefore to seek fresh alliances and to vacillate with France in the expedition that the French made towards the kingdom of Naples against the Spaniards, who were besieging Gaeta. His intention was to assure himself of them, which he would soon have succeeded in doing if Alexander had lived. These were the measures taken by him with regard to the present. As to the future, he feared that a new successor to the Church might not be friendly to him and might seek to deprive him of what Alexander had given him, and he sought to provide against this in four ways. Firstly, by destroying all who were of the blood of those ruling families which he had despoiled, in order to deprive the pope of any opportunity. Secondly, by gaining the friendship of the Roman nobles, so that he might through them hold as it were the pope in check. Thirdly, by obtaining as great a hold on the College as he could. Fourthly, by acquiring such power before the pope died as to be able to resist alone the first onslaught. Of these four things he had at the death of Alexander accomplished three, and the fourth he had almost accomplished.

For of the dispossessed rulers he killed as many as he could lay hands on, and very few escaped; he had gained to his party the Roman nobles; and he had a great share in the College. As to new possessions, he designed to become lord of Tuscany, and already possessed Perugia and Piombino, and had assumed the protectorate over Pisa; and as he had no longer to fear the French (for the French had been deprived of the kingdom of Naples by the Spaniards in such a way that both parties were obliged to buy his friendship) he seized Pisa. After this, Lucca and Siena at once yielded, partly through envy of the Florentines and partly through fear; the Florentines had no resources, so that, had he succeeded as he had done before, in the very year that Alexander died he would have gained such strength and renown as to be able to maintain himself without depending on the fortunes or strength of others, but solely by his own power and ability. But Alexander died five years after he had first drawn his sword. He left him with the state of Romagna only firmly established, and all the other schemes in mid-air, between two very powerful and hostile armies, and suffering from a fatal illness. But the valour and ability of the duke were such, and he knew so well how to win over men or vanquish them, and so strong were the foundations that he had laid in this short time, that if he had not had those two armies upon him, or else had been in good health, he would have survived every difficulty. And that his foundations were good is seen from the fact that the Romagna waited for him more than a month; in Rome, although half dead, he remained secure, and although the Baglioni, Vitelli, and Orsini entered Rome they found no followers against him. He was able, if not to make pope whom he wished, at any rate to prevent a pope being created whom he did not wish. But if at the death of Alexander he had been well everything would have been easy. And he told me on the day that Pope Julius II. was created, that he had thought of everything which might happen on the death of his father, and provided against everything, except that he had never thought that at his father's death he would be dying himself. Reviewing thus all the actions of the duke, I find nothing to blame, on the contrary, I feel bound, as I have done, to hold him up as an example to be imitated by all who by fortune and with the arms of others have risen to power. For with his great courage and high ambition he could not have acted otherwise, and his designs were only frustrated by the short life of Alexander and his own illness.

Whoever, therefore, deems it necessary in his new principality to secure himself against enemies, to gain friends, to conquer by force or fraud, to make himself beloved and feared by the people, followed and reverenced by the soldiers, to destroy those who can and may injure him, introduce innovations into old customs, to be severe and kind, magnanimous and liberal, suppress the old militia, create a new one, maintain the friendship of kings and princes in such a way that they are glad to benefit him and fear to injure him, such a one can find no better example than the actions of this man. The only thing he can be accused of is that in the creation of Julius II. he made a bad choice; for, as has been said, not being able to choose his own pope, he could still prevent any one being made pope, and he ought never to have permitted any of those cardinals to be raised to the papacy whom he had injured, or who when pope would stand in fear of him. For men commit injuries either through fear or through hate.

Those whom he had injured were, among others, San Pietro ad Vincula, Colonna, San Giorgio, and Ascanio. All the others, if assumed to the pontificate, would have had to fear him except Rohan and the Spaniards; the latter through their relationship and obligations to him, the former from his great power, being related to the King of France. For these reasons the duke ought above all things to have created a Spaniard pope; and if unable to, then he should have consented to Rohan being appointed and not San Pietro ad Vincula. And whoever thinks that in high personages new benefits cause old offences to be forgotten, makes a great mistake. The duke, therefore, erred in this choice, and it was the cause of his ultimate ruin.

VIII. OF THOSE WHO HAVE ATTAINED THE POSITION OF PRINCE BY VILLAINY

But as there are still two ways of becoming prince which cannot be attributed entirely either to fortune or to ability, they must not be passed over, although one of them could be more fully discussed if we were treating of republics. These are when one becomes prince by some nefarious or villainous means, or when a private citizen becomes the prince of his country through the favour of his fellow-citizens.

And in speaking of the former means, I will give two examples, one ancient, the other modern, without entering further into the merits of this method, as I judge them to be sufficient for any one obliged to imitate them. Agathocles the Sicilian rose not only from private life but from the lowest and most abject position to be King of Syracuse. The son of a potter, he led a life of the utmost wickedness through all the stages of his fortune. Nevertheless, his wickedness was accompanied by such vigour of mind and body that, having joined the militia, he rose through all its grades to be prætor of Syracuse. Having been appointed to this position, and having decided to become prince, and to hold with violence and without the support of others that which had been granted him; and having imparted his design to Hamilcar the Carthaginian, who with his armies was fighting in Sicily, he called together one morning the people and senate of Syracuse, as if he had to deliberate on matters of importance to the republic, and at a given signal had all the senators and the richest men of the people killed by his soldiers; after their death he occupied and held rule over the city without any civil disorders. And although he was twice beaten by the Carthaginians and ultimately besieged, he was able not only to defend the city, but leaving a portion of his forces for its defence, with the remainder he invaded Africa, and in a short time liberated Syracuse from the siege and brought the Carthaginians to great extremities, so that they were obliged to come to terms with him, and remain contented with the possession of Africa, leaving Sicily to Agathocles. Whoever considers, therefore, the actions and qualities of this man, will see few if any things which can be attributed to fortune; for, as above stated, it was not by the favour of any person, but through the grades of the militia, which he had gained with a thousand hardships and perils, that he arrived at the position of prince, which he afterwards maintained by so many courageous and perilous expedients. It cannot be called a virtue to kill one's fellow-citizens, betray one's friends, be without faith, without pity, and without religion, by which methods one may indeed gain an empire, but not glory. For if the virtues of Agathocles in braving and overcoming perils, and his greatness of soul in supporting and surmounting obstacles be considered, one sees no reason for holding him inferior to any of the most renowned captains. Nevertheless his barbarous cruelty and inhumanity, together with his countless atrocities, do not permit of his being named among the most famous men. We cannot attribute to fortune or merit that which he achieved without either. In our own times, during the reign of Alexander VI., Oliverotto du Fermo had been left a young boy under the care of his maternal uncle, Giovanni Fogliani, who brought him up, and sent him in early youth to fight under Paolo Vitelli, in order that he might, under that discipline, obtain a good military position. On the death of Paolo he fought under his brother Vitellozzo, and in a very short time, being of great intelligence, and active in mind and body, he became one of the leaders of his troops. But deeming it servile to be under others, he resolved, with the help of some citizens of Fermo, who preferred servitude to the liberty of their country, and with the favour of the Vitellis, to occupy Fermo; he therefore wrote to Giovanni Fogliani, how, having been for many years away from home, he wished to come to see him and his city, and in some measure to revisit his estates. And as he had only laboured to gain honour, in order that his fellow-citizens might see that he had not spent his time in vain, he wished to come honourably accompanied by one hundred horsemen, his friends and followers, and prayed him that he would be pleased to order that he should be received with honour by the citizens of Fermo, by which he would honour not only him, Oliverotto, but also himself, as he had been his pupil. Giovanni did not fail in any duty towards his nephew; he caused him to be honourably received by the people of Fermo, and lodged him in his own houses. After waiting some days to arrange all that was necessary to his villainous projects, Oliverotto invited Giovanni Fogliani and all the principal men of Fermo to a grand banquet. After the dinner and the entertainments usual at such feasts, Oliverotto artfully introduced certain important matters of discussion, speaking of the greatness of Pope Alexander, and of his son Cesare, and of their enterprises. To which discourses Giovanni and others having replied, he all at once rose, saying that these matters should be spoken of in a more secret place, and withdrew into a room where Giovanni and the other citizens followed him. They were no sooner seated than soldiers rushed out of hiding-places and killed Giovanni and all the others. After which massacre Oliverotto mounted his horse, rode through the town and besieged the chief magistrate in his palace, so that through fear they were obliged to obey him and form a government, of which he made himself prince. And all those being dead who, if discontented, could injure him, he fortified himself with new orders, civil and military, in such a way that within the year that he held the principality he was not only safe himself in the city of Fermo, but had become formidable to all his neighbours. And his overthrow would have been difficult, like that of Agathocles, if he had not allowed himself to be deceived by Cesare Borgia, when he besieged the Orsinis and Vitellis at Sinigaglia, as already related, where he also was taken, one year after the parricide he had committed, and strangled, together with Vitellozzo, who had been his teacher in ability and atrocity. Some may wonder how it came about that Agathocles, and others like him, could, after infinite treachery and cruelty, live secure for many years in their country and defend themselves from external enemies without being conspired against by their subjects; although many others have, through their cruelty, been unable to maintain their position in times of peace, not to speak of the uncertain times of war.

I believe this arises from the cruelties being used well or badly. Well used may be called those (if it is permissible to use the word well of evil) which are committed once for the need of securing one's self, and which afterwards are not persisted in, but are exchanged for measures as useful to the subjects as possible. Cruelties ill-used are those which, although at first few, increase rather than diminish with time. Those who follow the former method may remedy in some measure their condition, both with God and man; as did Agathocles. As to the others, it is impossible for them to maintain themselves. Whence it is to be noted, that in taking a state the conqueror must arrange to commit all his cruelties at once, so as not to have to recur to them every day, and so as to be able, by not making fresh changes, to reassure people and win them over by benefiting them. Whoever acts otherwise, either through timidity or bad counsels, is always obliged to stand with knife in hand, and can never depend on his subjects, because they, through continually fresh injuries, are unable to depend upon him. For injuries should be done all together, so that being less tasted, they will give less offence. Benefits should be granted little by little, so that they may be better enjoyed. And above all, a prince must live with his subjects in such a way that no accident should make him change it, for good or evil; for necessity arising in adverse times, you are not in time with severity, and the good that you do does not profit you, as it is judged to be forced, and you will derive no benefit whatever from it.

IX. OF THE CIVIC PRINCIPALITY

But we now come to the case where a citizen becomes prince not through crime or intolerable violence, but by the favour of his fellow-citizens, which may be called a civic principality. To arrive at this position depends not entirely on worth or entirely on fortune, but rather on cunning assisted by fortune. One attains it by help of popular favour or by the favour of the aristocracy. For in every city these two opposite parties are to be found, arising from the desire of the populace to avoid the oppression of the great, and the desire of the great to command and oppress the people. And from these two opposing interests arises in the city one of three effects: either absolute government, liberty, or license. The former is created either by the populace or the nobility depending on the relative opportunities of the two parties; for when the nobility see that they are unable to resist the people they unite in creating one of their number prince, so as to be able to carry out their own designs under the shadow of his authority. The populace, on the other hand, when unable to resist the nobility, endeavour to create a prince in order to be protected by his authority. He who becomes prince by help of the nobility has greater difficulty in maintaining his power than he who is raised by the populace, for he is surrounded by those who think themselves his equals, and is thus unable to direct or command as he pleases. But one who is raised to the leadership by popular favour finds himself alone, and has no one or very few who are not ready to obey him. Besides which, it is impossible to satisfy the nobility by fair dealing and without inflicting injury on others, whereas it is very easy to satisfy the mass of the people in this way. For the aim of the people is more honest than that of the nobility, the latter desiring to oppress, and the former merely to avoid oppression. It must also be added that the prince can never insure himself against a hostile populace on account of their number, but he can against the hostility of the great, as they are but few. The worst that a prince has to expect from a hostile people is to be abandoned, but from hostile nobles he has to fear not only abandonment but their active opposition, and as they are more farseeing and more cunning, they are always in time to save themselves and take sides with the one who they expect will conquer. The prince is, moreover, obliged to live always with the same people, but he can easily do without the same nobility, being able to make and unmake them at any time, and increase their position or deprive them of it as he pleases. And to throw further light on this part, I would say, that the nobles are to be considered in two different manners; that is, they are either to be ruled so as to make them entirely depend on your fortunes, or else not. Those that are thus bound to you and are not rapacious, must be honoured and loved; those who are not bound must be considered in two ways, they either do this through pusillanimity and natural want of courage, and in this case you ought to make use of them, and especially such as are of good counsel, so that they may honour you in prosperity and in adversity you have not to fear them. But when they are not bound to you of set purpose and for ambitious ends, it is a sign that they think more of themselves than of you; and from such men the prince must guard himself and look upon them as secret enemies, who will help to ruin him when in adversity. One, however, who becomes prince by favour of the populace, must maintain its friendship, which he will find easy, the people asking nothing but not to be oppressed. But one who against the people's wishes becomes prince by favour of the nobles, should above all endeavour to gain the favour of the people; this will be easy to him if he protects them. And as men, who receive good from those they expected evil from, feel under a greater obligation to their benefactor, so the subject populace will become even better disposed towards him than if he had become prince through their favour. The prince can win their favour in many ways, which vary according to circumstances, for which no certain rule can be given, and will therefore be passed over.

I will only say, in conclusion, that it is necessary for a prince to possess the friendship of the people; otherwise he has no resource in times of adversity. Nabis, prince of the Spartans, sustained a siege by the whole of Greece and a victorious Roman army, and defended against them his country and maintained his own position. It sufficed when the danger arose for him to make sure of a few, which would not have been enough if the populace had been hostile to him. And let no one oppose my opinion in this by quoting the trite proverb, "He who builds on the people, builds on mud"; because that is true when a private citizen relies upon the people and persuades himself that they will liberate him if he is oppressed by enemies or by the magistrates; in this case he might often find himself deceived, as happened in Rome to the Gracchi and in Florence to Messer Georgio Scali.

But when it is a prince who founds himself on this basis, one who can command and is a man of courage, and does not get frightened in adversity, and does not neglect other preparations, and one who by his own courage and measures animates the mass of the people, he will not find himself deceived by them, and he will find that he has laid his foundations well. Usually these principalities are in danger when the prince from the position of a civil ruler changes to an absolute one, for these princes either command themselves or by means of magistrates. In the latter case their position is weaker and more dangerous, for they are at the mercy of those citizens who are appointed magistrates, who can, especially in times of adversity, with great facility deprive them of their position, either by acting against them or by not obeying them. The prince is not in time, in such dangers, to assume absolute authority, for the citizens and subjects who are accustomed to take their orders from the magistrates are not ready in these emergencies to obey his, and he will always in doubtful times lack men whom he can rely on. Such a prince cannot base himself on what he sees in quiet times, when the citizens have need of the state; for then every one is full of promises and each one is ready to die for him when death is far off; but in adversity, when the state has need of citizens, then he will find but few. And this experience is the more dangerous, in that it can only be had once. Therefore a wise prince will seek means by which his subjects will always and in every possible condition of things have need of his government, and then they will always be faithful to him.

X. HOW THE STRENGTH OF ALL STATES SHOULD BE MEASURED

In examining the character of these principalities it is necessary to consider another point, namely, whether the prince has such a position as to be able in case of need to maintain himself alone, or whether he has always need of the protection of others. The better to explain this I would say, that I consider those capable of maintaining themselves alone who can, through abundance of men or money, put together a sufficient army, and hold the field against any one who assails them; and I consider to have need of others, those who cannot take the field against their enemies, but are obliged to take refuge within their walls and stand on the defensive. We have already discussed the former case and will speak in future of it as occasion arises. In the second case there is nothing to be said except to encourage such a prince to provision and fortify his own town, and not to trouble about the country. And whoever has strongly fortified his town and, as regards the government of his subjects, has proceeded as we have already described and will further relate, will be attacked with great reluctance, for men are always averse to enterprises in which they foresee difficulties, and it can never appear easy to attack one who has his town well-guarded and is not hated by the people. The cities of Germany are extremely liberal, have little surrounding country, and obey the emperor when they choose, and they do not fear him or any other potentate that they have about them. They are fortified in such a manner that every one thinks that to reduce them would be tedious and difficult, for they all have the necessary moats and bastions, sufficient artillery, and always keep in the public storehouses food and drink and fuel for one year. Beyond which, to keep the lower classes satisfied, and without loss to the public, they have always enough means to give them work for one year in these employments which form the nerve and life of the town, and in the industries by which the lower classes live; military exercises are still held in reputation, and many regulations are in force for maintaining them. A prince, therefore, who possesses a strong city and does not make himself hated, cannot be assaulted; and if he were to be so, the assailant would be obliged to retire shamefully; for so many things change, that it is almost impossible for any one to hold the field for a year with his armies idle. And to those who urge that the people, having their possessions outside and seeing them burnt, will not have patience, and the long siege and self-interest will make them forget their prince, I reply that a powerful and courageous prince will always overcome those difficulties by now raising the hopes of his subjects that the evils will not last long, now impressing them with fear of the enemy's cruelty, now by dexterously assuring himself of those who appear too bold. Besides which, the enemy would naturally burn and ruin the country on first arriving and in the time when men's minds are still hot and eager to defend themselves, and therefore the prince has still less to fear, for after some days, when people have cooled down, the damage is done, the evil has been suffered, and there is no remedy, so that they are the more ready to unite with their prince, as it appears that he is under an obligation to them, their houses having been burnt and their possessions ruined in his defence.

It is the nature of men to be us much bound by the benefits that they confer as by those they receive. From which it follows that, everything considered, a prudent prince will not find it difficult to uphold the courage of his subjects both at the commencement and during a state of siege, if he possesses provisions and means to defend himself.

XI. OF ECCLESIASTICAL PRINCIPALITIES

It now remains to us only to speak of ecclesiastical principalities, with regard to which the difficulties lie wholly before they are possessed. They are acquired either by ability or by fortune; but are maintained without either, for they are sustained by the ancient religious customs, which are so powerful and of such quality, that they keep their princes in power in whatever manner they proceed and live. These alone have a state without defending it, have subjects without governing them, and the states, not being defended, are not taken from them; the subjects not being governed do not disturb themselves, and neither think of nor are capable of alienating themselves from them. Only these principalities, therefore, are secure and happy. But as they are upheld by higher causes, which the human mind cannot attain to, I will abstain from speaking of them; for being exalted and maintained by God, it would be the work of a presumptuous and foolish man to discuss them.

However, I might be asked how it has come about that the Church has reached such great temporal power, when, previous to Alexander VI., the Italian potentates,—and not merely the really powerful ones, but every lord or baron, however insignificant, held it in slight esteem as regards temporal power; whereas now it is dreaded by a king of France, whom it has been able to drive out of Italy, and has also been able to ruin the Venetians. Therefore, although this is well known, I do not think it superfluous to call it to mind. Before Charles, King of France, came into Italy, this country was under the rule of the pope, the Venetians, the King of Naples, the Duke of Milan, and the Florentines. These potentates had to have two chief cares: one, that no foreigner should enter Italy by force of arms, the other that none of the existing governments should extend its dominions. Those chiefly to be watched were the pope and the Venetians. To keep back the Venetians required the ruin of all the others, as in the defence of Ferrara, and to keep down the pope they made use of the Roman barons. These were divided into two factions, the Orsinis and the Colonnas, and as there was constant quarrelling between them, and they were constantly under arms, before the eyes of the pope, they kept the papacy weak and infirm. And although there arose now and then a resolute pope like Sextus, yet his fortune or ability was never able to liberate him from these evils. The shortness of their life was the reason of this, for in the course of ten years which, as a general rule, a pope lived, he had great difficulty in suppressing even one of the factions, and if, for example, a pope had almost put down the Colonnas, a new pope would succeed who was hostile to the Orsinis, which caused the Colonnas to spring up again, and he was not in time to suppress them. This caused the temporal power of the pope to be of little esteem in Italy.

Then arose Alexander VI. who of all the pontiffs who have ever reigned, best showed how a pope might prevail both by money and by force. With Duke Valentine as his instrument, and on the occasion of the French invasion, he did all that I have previously described in speaking of the actions of the duke. And although his object was to aggrandise not the Church but the duke, what he did resulted in the aggrandisement of the Church, which after the death of the duke became the heir of his labours. Then came Pope Julius, who found the Church powerful, possessing all Romagna, all the Roman barons suppressed, and the factions destroyed by the severity of Alexander. He also found the way open for accumulating wealth in ways never used before the time of Alexander. These measures were not only followed by Julius, but increased; he resolved to gain Bologna, put down the Venetians and drive the French from Italy, in all which enterprises he was successful. He merits the greater praise, as he did everything to increase the power of the Church and not of any private person. He also kept the Orsini and Colonna parties in the conditions in which he found them, and although there were some leaders among them who might have made changes, there were two things that kept them steady: one, the greatness of the Church, which they dreaded; the other, the fact that they had no cardinals, who are the origin of the tumults among them. For these parties are never at rest when they have cardinals, for these stir up the parties both within Rome and outside, and the barons are forced to defend them. Thus from the ambitions of prelates arise the discords and tumults among the barons. His holiness, Pope Leo X., therefore, has found the pontificate in a very powerful condition, from which it is hoped, that as those popes made it great by force of armies, so he through his goodness and infinite other virtues will make it both great and venerated.

XII. THE DIFFERENT KINDS OF MILITIA AND MERCENARY SOLDIERS

Having now discussed fully the qualities of these principalities of which I proposed to treat, and partially considered the causes of their prosperity or failure, and having also showed the methods by which many have sought to obtain such states, it now remains for me to treat generally of the methods of attack and defence that can be used in each of them. We have said already how necessary it is for a prince to have his foundations good, otherwise he is certain to be ruined. The chief foundations of all states, whether new, old, or mixed, are good laws and good arms. And as there cannot be good laws where there are not good arms, and where there are good arms there should be good laws, I will not now discuss the laws, but will speak of the arms. I say, therefore, that the arms by which a prince defends his possessions are either his own, or else mercenaries, or auxiliaries, or mixed. The mercenaries and auxiliaries are useless and dangerous, and if any one keeps his state based on the arms of mercenaries, he will never stand firm or sure, as they are disunited, ambitious, without discipline, faithless, bold amongst friends, cowardly amongst enemies, they have no fear of God, and keep no faith with men. Ruin is only deferred as long as the assault is postponed; in peace you are despoiled by them, and in war by the enemy. The cause of this is that they have no love or other motive to keep them in the field beyond a trifling wage, which is not enough to make them ready to die for you. They are quite willing to be your soldiers so long as you do not make war, but when war comes, it is either fly or be off. I ought to have little trouble in proving this, since the ruin of Italy is now caused by nothing else but through her having relied for many years on mercenary arms. These were somewhat improved in a few cases, and appeared courageous among themselves, but when the foreigner came they showed their worthlessness. Thus it came about that King Charles of France was allowed to take Italy without the slightest trouble, and those who said that it was owing to our sins, spoke the truth, but it was not the sins that they believed but those that I have related. And as it was the sins of princes, they too have suffered the punishment. I will explain more fully the defects of these arms. Mercenary captains are either very capable men or not; if they are, you cannot rely upon them, for they will always aspire to their own greatness, either by oppressing you, their master, or by oppressing others against your intentions; but if the captain is not an able man, he will generally ruin you. And if it is replied to this, that whoever has armed forces will do the same, whether these are mercenary or not, I would reply that as armies are to be used either by a prince or by a republic, the prince must go in person to take the position of captain, and the republic must send its own citizens. If the one sent turns, out incompetent, it must change him; and if capable, keep him by law from going beyond the proper limits. And it is seen by experience that only princes and armed republics make very great progress, whereas mercenary forces do nothing but damage, and also an armed republic submits less easily to the rule of one of its citizens than a republic armed by foreign forces. Rome and

Sparta were for many centuries well-armed and free. The Swiss are well armed and enjoy great freedom. As an example of mercenary armies in antiquity there are the Carthaginians, who were oppressed by their mercenary soldiers, after the termination of the first war with the Romans, even while they still had their own citizens as captains. Philip of Macedon was made captain of their forces by the Thebans after the death of Epaminondas, and after gaining the victory he deprived them of liberty. The Milanese, on the death of Duke Philip, hired Francesco Sforza against the Venetians, who having overcome the enemy at Caravaggio, allied himself with them to oppress the Milanese his employers. The father of this Sforza, being a soldier in the service of the Queen Giovanna of Naples, left her suddenly unarmed, by which she was compelled, in order not to lose the kingdom, to throw herself into the arms of the King of Aragon. And if the Venetians and Florentines have in times past increased their dominions by means of such forces, and their captains have not made themselves princes but have defended them, I reply that the Florentines in this case have been favoured by chance, for of the capable leaders whom they might have feared, some did not conquer, some met with opposition, and others directed their ambition elsewhere. The one who did not conquer was Sir John Hawkwood, whose fidelity could not be known as he was not victorious, but every one will admit that, had he conquered, the Florentines would have been at his mercy. Sforza had always the Bracceschi against him, they being constantly at enmity. Francesco directed his ambition towards Lombardy; Braccio against the Church and the kingdom of

Naples. But let us look at what followed a short time ago. The Florentines appointed Paolo Vitelli their captain, a man of great prudence, who had risen from a private station to the highest reputation. If he had taken Pisa no one can deny that it was highly important for the Florentines to retain his friendship, because had he become the soldier of their enemies they would have had no means of opposing him; and in order to retain him they would have been obliged to obey him. As to the Venetians, if one considers the progress they made, it will be seen that they acted surely and gloriously so long as they made war with their own forces; that it was before they commenced their enterprises on land that they fought courageously with their own gentlemen and armed populace, but when they began to fight on land they abandoned this virtue, and began to follow the Italian custom. And at the commencement of their land conquests they had not much to fear from their captains, their land possessions not being very large, and their reputation being great, but as their possessions increased, as they did under Carmagnola, they had an example of their mistake. For seeing that he was very powerful, after he had defeated the Duke of Milan, and knowing, on the other hand, that he was not enterprising in warfare, they considered that they would not make any more conquests with him, and they neither would nor could dismiss him, for fear of losing what they had already gained. They were therefore obliged, in order to make sure of him, to have him killed. They then had for captains Bartolommeo da Bergamo, Roberto da San Severino, Count di Pitigliano, and such like, from whom they had to fear loss instead of gain, as happened subsequently at Vailà, where in one day they lost what they had laboriously gained in eight hundred years; for with these forces, only slow and trifling acquisitions are made, but sudden and miraculous losses. And as I have cited these examples from Italy, which has now for many years been governed by mercenary forces, I will now deal more largely with them, so that having seen their origin and progress, they can be better remedied. You must understand that in these latter times, as soon as the empire began to be repudiated in Italy and the pope to gain greater reputation in temporal matters, Italy was divided into many states; many of the principal cities took up arms against their nobles, who, favoured by the emperor, had held them in subjection, and the Church encouraged this in order to increase its temporal power. In many other cities one of the inhabitants became prince. Thus Italy having fallen almost entirely into the hands of the Church and a few republics, and the priests and other citizens not being accustomed to bear arms, they began to hire foreigners as soldiers. The first to bring reputation for this kind of militia was Alberigo da Como, a native of Romagna. The discipline of this man produced, among others, Braccio and Sforza, who were in their day the arbiters of Italy. After these came all those others who up to the present day have commanded the armies of Italy, and the result of their prowess has been that Italy has been overrun by Charles, preyed on by Louis, tyrannised over by Ferrando, and insulted by the Swiss. The system adopted by them was, in the first place, to increase their own reputation by discrediting the infantry. They did this because, as they had no country and lived on their earnings, a few foot soldiers did not augment their reputation, and they could not maintain a large number and therefore they restricted themselves almost entirely to cavalry, by which with a smaller number they were well paid and honoured. They reduced things to such a state that in an army of 20,000 soldiers there were not 2000 foot. They had also used every means to spare themselves and the soldiers any hardship or fear by not killing each other in their encounters, but taking prisoners without a blow. They made no attacks on fortifications by night; and those in the fortifications did not attack the tents at night, they made no stockades on ditches round their camps, and did not take the field in winter. All these things were permitted by their military rules, and adopted, as we have said, to avoid trouble and danger, so that they have reduced Italy to slavery and degradation.

XIII. OF AUXILIARY, MIXED, AND NATIVE TROOPS

Auxiliary forces, which are the other kind of useless forces, are when one calls on a potentate to come and aid one with his troops, as was done in recent times by Julius, who seeing the wretched failure of his mercenary forces, in his Ferrara enterprise, had recourse to auxiliaries, and arranged with Ferrando, King of Spain, that he should help him with his armies. These forces may be good in themselves, but they are always dangerous for those who borrow them, for if they lose you are defeated, and if they conquer you remain their prisoner. And although ancient history is full of examples of this, I will not depart from the example of Pope Julius II., which is still fresh. Nothing could be less prudent than the course he adopted; for, wishing to take Ferrara, he put himself entirely into the power of a foreigner. But by good fortune there arose a third cause which prevented him reaping the effects of his bad choice; for when his auxiliaries were beaten at Ravenna, the Swiss rose up and drove back the victors, against all expectation of himself or others, so that he was not taken prisoner by the enemy which had fled, nor by his own auxiliaries, having conquered by other arms than theirs. The Florentines, being totally disarmed, hired 10,000 Frenchmen to attack Pisa, by which measure they ran greater risk than at any period of their struggles. The emperor of Constantinople, to oppose his neighbours, put 10,000 Turks into Greece, who after the war would not go away again, which was the beginning of the servitude of Greece to the infidels. Any one, therefore, who wishes not to conquer, would do well to use these forces, which are much more dangerous than mercenaries, as with them ruin is complete, for they are all united, and owe obedience to others, whereas with mercenaries, when they have conquered, it requires more time and a good opportunity for them to injure you, as they do not form a single body and have been engaged and paid by you, therefore a third party that you have made leader cannot at once acquire enough authority to be able to injure you. In a word, the greatest dangers with mercenaries lies in their cowardice and reluctance to fight, but with auxiliaries the danger lies in their courage. A wise prince, therefore, always avoids these forces and has recourse to his own, and would prefer rather to lose with his own men than conquer with the forces of others, not deeming it a true victory which is gained by foreign arms. I never hesitate to cite the example of Cesare Borgia and his actions. This duke entered Romagna with auxiliary troops, leading forces composed entirely of French soldiers, and with these he took Imola and Forli; but as they seemed unsafe, he had recourse to mercenaries, and hired the Orsini and Vitelli; afterwards finding these uncertain to handle, unfaithful and dangerous, he suppressed them, and relied upon his own men. And the difference between these forces can be easily seen if one considers the difference between the reputation of the duke when he had only the French, when he had the Orsini and Vitelli, and when he had to rely on himself and his own soldiers. His reputation will be found to have constantly increased, and he was never so highly esteemed as when every one saw that he was the sole master of his forces.

I do not wish to go away from recent Italian instances, but I cannot omit Hiero of Syracuse, whom I have already mentioned. This man being, as I said, made head of the army by the Syracusans, immediately recognised the uselessness of that mercenary militia which was composed like our Italian mercenary troops, and as he thought it unsafe either to retain them or dismiss them, he had them cut in pieces and thenceforward made war with his own arms and not those of others. I would also call to mind a figure out of the Old Testament which well illustrates this point. When David offered to Saul to go and fight with the Philistine champion Goliath, Saul, to encourage him, armed him with his own arms, which when David had tried on he refused saying, that with them he could not fight so well; he preferred, therefore, to face the enemy with his own sling and knife. In short, the arms of others either fall away from you, or overburden you, or else impede you. Charles VIII., father of King Louis XL, having through good fortune and bravery liberated France from the English, recognised this necessity of being armed with his own forces, and established in his kingdom a system of men-at-arms and infantry. Afterwards King Louis his son abolished the infantry and began to hire Swiss, which mistake being followed by others is, as may now be seen, a cause of danger to that kingdom. For by giving such reputation to the Swiss, France has disheartened all her own troops, the infantry having been abolished and the men-at-arms being obliged to foreigners for assistance; for being accustomed to fight with Swiss troops, they think they cannot conquer without them. Whence it comes that the French are insufficiently strong to oppose the Swiss, and without the aid of the Swiss they will not venture against others. The armies of the French are thus of a mixed kind, partly mercenary and partly her own; taken together they are much better than troops entirely composed of mercenaries or auxiliaries, but much inferior to national forces.

XIV. WHAT THE DUTIES OF A PRINCE ARE WITH REGARD TO THE MILITIA

A Prince should therefore have no other aim or thought, nor take up any other thing for his study, but war and its order and discipline, for that is the only art that is necessary to one who commands, and it is of such virtue that it not only maintains those who are born princes, but often enables men of private fortune to attain to that rank. And one sees, on the other hand, that when princes think more of luxury than of arms, they lose their state. The chief cause which makes any one lose it, is the contempt of this art, and the way to acquire it is to be well versed in the same. Francesco Sforza, through being well armed, became, from a private position, Duke of Milan; his sons, through wishing to avoid the fatigue and hardship of war, from dukes became private persons. For among other evils caused by being disarmed, it renders you contemptible; which is one of those disgraceful things which a prince must guard against, as will be explained later. Because there is no comparison whatever between an armed man and a disarmed one; it is not reasonable to suppose that one who is armed will obey willingly one who is unarmed; or that any unarmed man will remain safe among armed servants. For one being disdainful and the other suspicious, it is not possible for them to act well together. And yet a prince who is ignorant of military matters, besides the other misfortunes already mentioned, cannot be esteemed by his soldiers, nor have confidence in them. He ought, therefore, never to let his thoughts stray from the exercise of war; and in peace he ought to practise it more than in war, which he can do in two ways: both by action and by study. As to action, he must, besides keeping his men well-disciplined and exercised, engage continually in hunting, and thus accustom his body to hardships; and on the other hand learn the nature of the land, how the mountains rise, how the valleys are disposed, where the plains lie, and understand the nature of the rivers and swamps, and to this he should devote great attention. This knowledge is useful in two ways. In the first place, one learns to know one's country, and can the better see how to defend it. Then by means of the knowledge and experience gained in one locality, one can easily understand any other that it may be necessary to venture on, for the hills and valleys, plains and rivers of Tuscany, for instance, have a certain resemblance to those of other provinces, so that from a knowledge of the country in one province one can easily arrive at a knowledge of others. And that prince who is lacking in this skill is wanting in the first essentials of a leader; for it is this which teaches how to find the enemy, take up quarters, lead armies, arrange marches and occupy positions with advantage. Philopœmen, prince of the Achæi, among other praises bestowed on him by writers, is lauded because in times of peace he thought of nothing but the methods of warfare, and when he was in the country with his friends, he often stopped and asked them: If the enemy were on that hill and we found ourselves here with our army, which of us would have the advantage? How could we safely approach him maintaining our order? If we wished to retire, what ought we to do? If they retired, how should we follow them? And he put before them as they went along all the cases that might happen to an army, heard their opinion, gave his own, fortifying it by argument; so that through these continued cogitations there could never happen any incident when leading his armies for which he was not prepared. But as to exercise for the mind, the prince ought to read history and study the actions of eminent men, see how they acted in warfare, examine the causes of their victories and losses in order to imitate the former and avoid the latter, and above all, do as some eminent men have done in the past, who have imitated some one, who has been much praised and glorified, and have always kept their deeds and actions before them, as they say Alexander the Great imitated Achilles, Cæsar Alexander, and Scipio Cyrus. And whoever reads the life of Cyrus written by Xenophon, will perceive in the life of Scipio how gloriously he imitated him, and how, in chastity, affability, humanity, and liberality Scipio conformed to those qualities of Cyrus described by Xenophon.

A wise prince should follow similar methods and never remain idle in peaceful times, but by industry make such good use of the time as may serve him in adversity, so that when fortune changes she may find him prepared to resist her blows.

XV. OF THE THINGS FOR WHICH MEN, AND ESPECIALLY PRINCES, ARE PRAISED OR BLAMED

It remains now to be seen what are the methods and rules for a prince as regards his subjects and friends. And as I know that many have written of this, I fear that my writing about it may be deemed presumptuous, differing as I do, especially in this matter, from the opinions of others. But my intention being to write something of use to those who understand it, it appears to me more proper to go to the real truth of the matter than to its imagination; and many have imagined republics and principalities which have never been seen or known to exist in reality; for how we live is so far removed from how we ought to live, that he who abandons what is done for what ought to be done, will rather learn to bring about his own ruin than his preservation. A man who wishes to make a profession of goodness in everything must necessarily come to grief among so many who are not good. Therefore it is necessary for a prince, who wishes to maintain himself, to learn how not to be good, and to use it and not use it according to the necessity of the case. Leaving on one side then those things which concern only an imaginary prince, and speaking of those that are real, I state that all men, when spoken of, and especially princes, who are placed at a greater height, are noted for some of those qualities which bring them either praise or blame. Thus one is considered liberal, another miserly; one a free giver, another rapacious; one cruel, another merciful; one a breaker of his word, another faithful; one effeminate and pusillanimous, another fierce and high-spirited; one humane, another proud; one lascivious, another chaste; one frank, another astute; one hard, another easy; one serious, another frivolous; one religious, another incredulous, and so on. I know that every one will admit that it would be highly praiseworthy in a prince to possess all the above-named qualities that are reputed good, but as they cannot all be possessed or observed, human conditions not permitting of it, it is necessary that he should be prudent enough to avoid the disgrace of those vices which would lose him the state, and guard himself against those which will not lose it him, if possible, but if not able to, he can indulge them with less scruple. And yet he must not mind incurring the disgrace of those vices, without which it would be difficult to save the state, for if one considers well, it will be found that some things which seem virtues would, if followed, lead to one's ruin, and some others which appear vices result, if followed, in one's greater security and well being.

XVI. OF LIBERALITY AND MISERLINESS

Beginning now with the first qualities above named, I say that it would be well to be considered liberal; nevertheless liberality used in such a way that you are not feared will injure you, because if used virtuously and in the proper way, it will not be known, and you will not incur the disgrace of the contrary vice. But one who wishes to obtain the reputation of liberality among men, must not omit every kind of sumptuous display, and to such an extent that a prince of this character will consume by such means all his resources, and will be at last compelled, if he wishes to maintain his name for liberality, to impose heavy charges on his people, become an extortioner, and do everything possible to obtain money. This will make his subjects begin to hate him and he will be little esteemed being poor, so that having by this liberality injured many and benefited but few, he will feel the first little disturbance and be endangered by every accident. If he recognises this and wishes to change his system, he incurs at once the charge of niggardliness; a prince, therefore, not being able to exercise this virtue of liberality without risk if it is known, must not, if he is prudent, object to be called miserly. In course of time he will be thought more liberal, when it is seen that by his parsimony his revenue is sufficient, that he can defend himself against those who make war on him, and undertake enterprises without burdening his people, so that he is really liberal to all those from whom he does not take, who are infinite in number, and miserly to all to whom he does not give, who are few.

In our times we have seen nothing great done except by those who have been esteemed miserly; the others have all been ruined. Pope Julius II., although he had made use of a reputation for liberality in order to attain the papacy, did not seek to retain it afterwards, so that he might be able to make war on the King of France, and he earned on so many wars without imposing an extraordinary tax, because his extra expenses were covered by the parsimony he had so long practised. The present King of Spain, if he had been thought liberal, would not have engaged in and won so many enterprises. For these reasons a prince must care little for the reputation of being a miser, if he wishes to avoid robbing his subjects, if he wishes to be able to defend himself, to not become poor and contemptible, and not to be forced to become rapacious; this vice of miserliness is one of those vices which enable him to reign. If it is said that Cæsar attained the empire through liberality, and that many others have reached the highest positions through being liberal or being thought so, I would reply that you are either a prince already or else on the way to become one. In the first case, this liberality is harmful; in the second, it is certainly necessary to be considered liberal, and Cæsar was one of those who wished to attain the mastery over Rome, but if after attaining it he had lived and had not moderated his expenses, he would have destroyed that empire. And should any one reply that there have been many princes, who have done great things with their armies, who have been thought extremely liberal, I would answer by saying that the prince may either spend his own wealth and that of his subjects or the wealth of others. In the first case he must be sparing, but in the second he must not neglect to be very liberal. This liberality is very necessary to a prince who marches with his armies, and lives by plunder, sacking and extorting, and is dealing with the wealth of others, for without it he would not be followed by his soldiers. And you may be very generous indeed with what is not the property of yourself or your subjects, as were Cyrus, Cæsar, and Alexander; for spending the wealth of others will not diminish your reputation, but increase it, only spending your own resources will injure you. There is nothing which destroys itself so much as liberality, for by using it you lose the power of using it, and become either poor and despicable, or, to escape poverty, rapacious and hated. And of all things that a prince must guard against, the most important are being despicable or hated, and liberality will lead you to one or other of these conditions. It is, therefore, wiser to have the name of a miser, which produces disgrace without hatred, than to incur of necessity the name of being rapacious, which produces both disgrace and hatred.

XVII. OF CRUELTY AND CLEMENCY, AND WHETHER IT IS BETTER TO BE LOVED OR FEARED

Proceeding to the other qualities before named, I say that every prince must desire to be considered merciful and not cruel. He must, however, take care not to misuse this mercifulness. Cesare Borgia was considered cruel, but his cruelty had settled the Romagna, united it, and brought it peace and confidence. If this is considered a benefit, it will be seen that he was really much more merciful than the Florentine people, who, to avoid the name of cruelty, allowed Pistoia to be destroyed. A prince, therefore, must not mind incurring the charge of cruelty for the purpose of keeping his subjects united and confident; for, with a very few examples, he will be more merciful than those who, from excess of tenderness, allow disorders to arise, from whence spring murders and rapine; for these as a rule injure the whole community, while the executions carried out by the prince injure only one individual. And of all princes, it is impossible for a new prince to escape the name of cruel, new states being always full of dangers. Wherefore Virgil makes Dido excuse the inhumanity of her rule by its being new, where she says:

> Res dura, et regni novitas me
> talia cogunt
> Moliri, et late fines custode tueri.

Nevertheless, he must be cautious in believing and acting, and must not inspire fear of his own accord, and must proceed in a temperate manner with prudence and humanity, so that too much confidence does not render him incautious, and too much diffidence does not render him intolerant. From this arises the question whether it is better to be loved more than feared, or feared more than loved. The reply is, that one ought to be both feared and loved, but as it is difficult for the two to go together, it is much safer to be feared than loved, if one of the two has to be wanting. For it may be said of men in general that they are ungrateful, voluble, dissemblers, anxious to avoid danger, and covetous of gain; as long as you benefit them, they are entirely yours; they offer you their blood, their goods, their life, and their children, as I have before said, when the necessity is remote; but when it approaches, they revolt And the prince who has relied solely on their words, without making other preparations, is ruined, for the friendship which is gained by purchase and not through grandeur and nobility of spirit is merited but is not secured, and at times is not to be had. And men have less scruple in offending one who makes himself loved than one who makes himself feared; for love is held by a chain of obligation which, men being selfish, is broken whenever it serves their purpose; but fear is maintained by a dread of punishment which never fails. Still, a prince should make himself feared in such a way that if he does not gain love, he at any rate avoids hatred; for fear, and the absence of hatred may well go together, and will be always attained by one who abstains from interfering with the property of his citizens and subjects or with their women. And when he is obliged to take the life of any one, to do so when there is a proper justification and manifest reason for it; but above all he must abstain from taking the property of others, for men forget more easily the death of their father than the loss of their patrimony. Then also pretexts for seizing property are never wanting, and one who begins to live by rapine will always find some reason for taking the goods of others, whereas causes for taking life are rarer and more quickly destroyed. But when the prince is with his army and has a large number of soldiers under his control, then it is extremely necessary that he should not mind being thought cruel; for without, this reputation he could not keep an army united, or disposed to any duty.

Among the noteworthy actions of Hannibal is numbered this, that although he had an enormous army, composed of men of all nations and fighting in foreign countries, there never arose any dissension either among them or against the prince, either in good fortune or in bad. This could not be due to anything but his inhuman cruelty, which together with his infinite other virtues, made him always venerated and terrible in the sight of his soldiers, and without it his other virtues would not have sufficed to produce that effect. Thoughtless writers admire on the one hand his actions, and on the other blame the principal cause of them. And that it is true that his other virtues would not have sufficed may be seen from the case of Scipio (very rare not only in his own times, but in all times of which memory remains), whose armies rebelled against him in Spain, which arose from nothing but his excessive kindness, which allowed more license to the soldiers than was consonant with military discipline. He was reproached with this in the senate by Fabius Maximus, who called him a corrupter of the Roman militia.

The Locri having been destroyed by one of Scipio's officers were not revenged by him, nor was the insolence of that officer punished, simply by reason of his easy nature; so much so, that some one wishing to excuse him in the senate, said that there were many men who knew rather how not to err, than how to correct the errors of others. This disposition would in time have tarnished the fame and glory of Scipio had he persevered in it under the empire, but living under the rule of the senate this harmful quality was not only concealed but became a glory to him. I conclude, therefore, with regard to being feared and loved, that men love at their own free will, but fear at the will of the prince, and that a wise prince must rely on what is in his power and not on what is in the power of others, and he must only trouble himself to avoid incurring hatred, as has been explained.

XVIII. IN WHAT WAY PRINCES MUST KEEP FAITH

How laudable it is for a prince to keep good faith and live with integrity, and not with astuteness, every one knows. Still the experience of our times shows those princes to have done great things who have had little regard for good faith, and have been able by astuteness to confuse men's brains, and who have ultimately overcome those who have, made loyalty their foundation. You must know, then, that there are two methods of fighting, the one by law, the other by force: the first method is that of men, the second of beasts; but as the first method is often insufficient, one must have recourse to the second. It is therefore necessary to know well how to use both the beast and the man. This was covertly taught to princes by ancient writers, who relate how Achilles and many others of those princes were given to Chiron the centaur to be brought up, who kept them under his discipline; this system of having for teacher one who was half beast and half man is meant to indicate that a prince must know how to use both natures, and that the one without the other is not durable. A prince being thus obliged to know well how to act as a beast must imitate the fox and the lion, for the lion cannot protect himself from snares, and the fox cannot defend himself from wolves. One must therefore be a fox to recognise snares, and a lion to frighten wolves. Those that wish to be only lions do not understand this. Therefore, a prudent ruler ought not to keep faith when by so doing it would be against his interest, and when the reasons which made him bind himself no longer exist. If men were all good, this precept would not be a good one; but as they are bad, and would not observe their faith with you, so you are not bound to keep faith with them. Nor are legitimate grounds ever wanting to a prince to give colour to the non-fulfilment of his promise. Of this one could furnish an infinite number of modern examples, and show how many times peace has been broken, and how many promises rendered worthless, by the faithlessness of princes, and those that have been best able to imitate the fox have succeeded best. But it is necessary to be able to disguise this character well, and to be a great feigner and dissembler; and men are so simple and so ready to obey present necessities, that one who deceives will always find those who allow themselves to be deceived. I will only mention one modern instance. Alexander VI. did nothing else but deceive men, he thought of nothing else, and found the way to do it; no man was ever more able to give assurances, or affirmed things with stronger oaths, and no man observed them less; however, he always succeeded in his deceptions, as he knew well this side of the world. It is not, therefore, necessary for a prince to have all the above-named qualities, but it is very necessary to seem to have them. I would even be bold to say that to possess them and to always observe them is dangerous, but to appear to possess them is useful. Thus it is well to seem pious, faithful, humane, religious, sincere, and also to be so; but you must have the mind so watchful that when it is needful to be otherwise you may be able to change to the opposite qualities. And it must be understood that a prince, and especially a new prince, cannot observe all those things which are considered good in men, being often obliged, in order to maintain the state, to act against faith, against charity, against humanity, and against religion. And, therefore, he must have a mind disposed to adapt itself according to the wind, and as the variations of fortune dictate, and, as I said before, not deviate from what is good, if possible, but be able to do evil if necessitated. A prince must take great care that nothing goes out of his mouth which is not full of the above-named five qualities, and, to see and hear him, he should seem to be all faith, all integrity, all humanity, and all, religion. And nothing is more necessary than to seem to have this last quality, for men in general judge more by the eyes than by the hands, for every one can see, but very few have to feel. Everybody sees what you appear to be, few feel what you are, and those few will not dare to oppose themselves to the many, who have the majesty of the state to defend them; and in the actions of men, and especially of princes, from which there is no appeal, the end is everything.

Let a prince therefore aim at living and maintaining state the state, the means will always be judged honourable and praised by every one, for the vulgar is always taken by appearances and the result of things; and the world consists only of the vulgar, and the few find a place when the many have nothing to rest upon. A certain prince of the present time, whom it is well not to name, never does anything but preach peace and good faith, but he is really a great enemy to both, and either of them, had he observed them, would have lost him both state and reputation on many occasions.

XIX. THAT WE MUST AVOID BEING DESPISED AND HATED

But as I have now spoken of the most important of the qualities in question, I will now deal briefly with the rest on the general principle, that the prince must, as already stated, avoid those things which will make him hated or despised; and whenever he succeeds in this, he will have done his part, and will find no danger in other vices.

He will chiefly become hated, as I said, by being rapacious, and usurping the property and women of his subjects, which he must abstain from doing, and whenever one does not attack the property or honour of the generality of men, they will live contented; and one will only have to combat the ambition of a few, who can be easily held in check in many ways. He is rendered despicable by being thought changeable, frivolous, effeminate, timid, and irresolute; which a prince must guard against as a rock of danger, and manage so that his actions show grandeur, high courage, seriousness, and strength; and as to the government of his subjects, let his sentence be irrevocable, and let him adhere to his decisions so that no one may think of deceiving him or making him change. The prince who creates such an opinion of himself gets a great reputation, and it is very difficult to conspire against one who has a great reputation, and he will not easily be attacked, so long as it is known that he is esteemed and reverenced by his subjects. For a prince must have two kinds of fear: one internal as regards his subjects, one external as regards foreign powers. From the latter he can defend himself with good arms and good friends, and he will always have good friends if he has good arms; and internal matters will always remain quiet, if they are not perturbed by conspiracy; and even if external powers sought to foment one, if he has ruled and lived as I have described, he will always if he stands firm be able to sustain every shock, as I have shown that Nabis the Spartan did. But with regard to the subjects, if not acted on from outside, it is still to be feared lest they conspire in secret, from which the prince may guard himself well by avoiding hatred and contempt, and keeping the people satisfied with him, which it is necessary to accomplish, as has been related at length. And one of the most potent remedies that a prince has against conspiracies, is that of not being hated or despised by the mass of the people; for whoever conspires always believes that he will satisfy the people by the death of their prince; but if he thought to offend them by doing this, he would fear to engage in such an undertaking, for the difficulties that conspirators have to meet are infinite. Experience shows that there have been very many conspiracies, but few have turned out well, for whoever conspires cannot act alone, and cannot find companions except among those who are discontented; and as soon as you have disclosed your intention to a malcontent, you give him the means of satisfying himself, for by revealing it he can hope to secure everything he wants; to such an extent that seeing a certain gain by doing this, and seeing on the other hand only a doubtful one and full of danger, he must either be a rare friend to you or else a very bitter enemy to the prince if he keeps faith with you. And to reduce the matter to narrow limits, I say, that on the side of the conspirator there is nothing but fear, jealousy, suspicion, and dread of punishment which frightens him; and on the side of the prince there is the majesty of government, the laws, the protection of friends and of the state which guard him. When to these things are added the goodwill of the people, it is impossible that any one should have the temerity to conspire. For whereas generally a conspirator has to fear before the execution of his plot, in this case he must also fear afterwards, having the people for an enemy, when his crime is accomplished, and thus not being able to hope for any refuge. Numberless instances might be given of this, but I will content myself with one which took place within the memory of our fathers. Messer Annibale Bentivogli, Prince of Bologna, ancestor of the present Messer Annibale, was killed by the Canneschi, who conspired against him. He left no relations but Messer Giovanni, who was then an infant, but after the murder the people rose up and killed all the Canneschi. This arose from the popular goodwill that the house of Bentivogli enjoyed at that time in Bologna, which was so great that, as there was nobody left after the death of Annibale who could govern the state, the Bolognese hearing that there was one of the Bentivogli family in Florence, who had till then been thought the son of a blacksmith, came to fetch him and gave him the government of the city, and it was governed by him until Messer Giovanni was old enough to assume the government.

I conclude, therefore, that a prince need trouble little about conspiracies when the people are well disposed, but when they are hostile and hold him in hatred, then he must fear everything and everybody. Well-ordered states and wise princes have studied diligently not to drive the nobles to desperation, and to satisfy the populace and keep it contented, for this is one of the most important matters that a prince has to deal with. Among the kingdoms that are well ordered and governed in our time is France, and there we find numberless good institutions on which depend the liberty and security of the king; of these the chief is the parliament and its authority, because he who established that kingdom, knowing the ambition and insolence of the great nobles, and deeming it necessary to have a bit in their mouths to check them; and knowing on the other hand the hatred of the mass of the people to the great, based on fear, and wishing to secure them, did not wish to make this the special care of the king, to relieve him of the dissatisfaction that he might incur among the nobles by favouring the people, and among the people by favouring the nobles. He therefore established a third judge that, without direct charge of the king, kept in check the great and favoured the lesser people. Nor could any better or more prudent measure have been adopted, nor better precaution for the safety of the king and the kingdom. From which another notable rule can be drawn, that princes should let the carrying out of unpopular duties devolve on others, and bestow favours themselves. I conclude again by saying that a prince must esteem his nobles, but not make himself hated by the populace. It may perhaps seem to some, that considering the life and death of many Roman emperors that they are instances contrary to my opinion, finding that some who lived always nobly and showed great strength of character, nevertheless lost the empire, or were killed by their subjects who conspired against them. Wishing to answer these objections, I will discuss the qualities of some emperors, showing the cause of their ruin not to be at variance with what I have stated, and I will also partly consider the things to be noted by whoever reads the deeds of these times. I will content myself with taking all those emperors who succeeded to the empire from Marcus the philosopher to Maximinus; these were Marcus, Commodus his son, Pertinax, Heliogabalus, Alexander, and Maximinus. And the first thing to note is, that whereas other princes have only to contend against the ambition of the great and the insolence of the people, the Roman emperors had a third difficulty, that of having to support the cruelty and avarice of the soldiers, which was such a difficulty that it was the cause of the ruin of many, it being difficult to satisfy both the soldiers and the people. For the people love tranquillity, and therefore like princes who are pacific, but the soldiers prefer a prince of military spirit, who is insolent, cruel, and rapacious. They wish him to exercise these qualities on the people so that they may get double pay and give vent to their avarice and cruelty. Thus it came about that those emperors who, by nature or art, had not such a reputation as could keep both parties in check, invariably were ruined, and the greater number of them who were raised to the empire being new men, knowing the difficulties of these two opposite dispositions, confined themselves to satisfying the soldiers, and thought little of injuring the people. This choice was necessary, princes not being able to avoid being hated by some one. They must first try not to be hated by the mass of the people; if they cannot accomplish this they must use every means to escape the hatred of the most powerful parties. And therefore these emperors, who being new men had need of extraordinary favours, adhered to the soldiers more willingly than to the people; whether this, however, was of use to them or not, depended on whether the prince knew how to maintain his reputation with them.

From these causes it resulted that Marcus, Pertinax, and Alexander, being all of modest life, lovers of justice, enemies of cruelty, humane and benign, had all a sad ending except Marcus. Marcus alone lived and died in honour, because he succeeded to the empire by hereditary right and did not owe it either to the soldiers or to the people; besides which, possessing many virtues which made him revered, he kept both parties in their place as long as he lived and was never either hated or despised. But Pertinax was created emperor against the will of the soldiers, who being accustomed to live licentiously under Commodus, could not put up with the honest life to which Pertinax wished to limit them, so that having made himself hated, and to this contempt being added because he was old, he was ruined at the very beginning of his administration. Whence it may be seen that hatred is gained as much by good works as by evil, and therefore, as I said before, a prince who wishes to maintain the state is often forced to do evil, for when that party, whether populace, soldiery, or nobles, whichever it be that you consider necessary to you for keeping your position, is corrupt, you must follow its humour and satisfy it, and in that case good works will be inimical to you. But let us come to Alexander, who was of such goodness, that among other things for which he is praised, it is said that in the fourteen years that he reigned no one was put to death by him without a fair trial. Nevertheless, being considered effeminate, and a man who allowed himself to be ruled by his mother, and having thus fallen into contempt, the army conspired against him and killed him. Looking, on the other hand, at the qualities of Commodus, Severus, Antoninus, extremely cruel and rapacious; to satisfy the soldiers there was no injury which they would not inflict on the people, and all except Severus ended badly. Severus, however, had such abilities that by maintaining the soldiers friendly to him, he was able to reign happily, although he oppressed the people, for his virtues made him so admirable in the sight both of the soldiers and the people that the latter were, as it were, astonished and stupefied, while the former were respectful and contented. As the deeds of this ruler were great for a new prince, I will briefly show how well he could use the qualities of the fox and the lion, whose natures, as I said before, it is necessary for a prince to imitate. Knowing the sloth of the Emperor Julian, Severus, who was leader of the army in Slavonia, persuaded the troops that it would be well to go to Rome to avenge the death of Pertinax, who had been slain by the Imperial guard, and under this pretext, without revealing his aspirations to the throne, marched with his army to Rome and was in Italy before his design was known. On his arrival in Rome the senate elected him emperor through fear, and Julian died. There remained after this beginning two difficulties to be faced by Severus before he could obtain the whole control of the empire: one in Asia, where Nigrinus, head of the Asiatic armies, had declared himself emperor; the other in the west from Albinus, who also aspired to the empire. And as he judged it dangerous to show himself hostile to both, he decided to attack Nigrinus and deceive Albinus, to whom he wrote that having been elected emperor by the senate he wished to share that dignity with him; he sent him the title of Cæsar and, by deliberation of the senate, he was declared his colleague; all of which was accepted as true by Albinus. But when Severus had defeated and killed Nigrinus, and pacified things in the East, he returned to Rome and charged Albinus in the senate with having, unmindful of the benefits received from him, traitorously sought to assassinate him, and stated that he was therefore obliged to go and punish his ingratitude. He then went to France to meet him, and there deprived him of both his position and his life. Whoever examines in detail the actions of Severus, will find him to have been a very ferocious lion and an extremely astute fox, and will see him to have been feared and respected by all and not hated by the army; and will not be surprised that he, a new man, should have been able to hold the empire so well, since his great reputation defended him always from that hatred that his rapacity might have produced in the people. But Antoninus his son was also a man of great ability, and possessed qualities that rendered him admirable in the sight of the people and also made him popular with the soldiers, for he was a military man, capable of enduring the most extreme hardships, disdainful of delicate food, and every other luxury, which made him loved by all the armies. However, his ferocity and cruelty were so great and unheard of, through his having, after executing many private individuals, caused a large part of the population of Rome and all that of Alexandria to be killed, that he became hated by all the world and began to be feared by those about him to such an extent that he was finally killed by a centurion in the midst of his army. Whence it is to be noted that this kind of death, which proceeds from the deliberate action of a determined man, cannot be avoided by princes, since any one who does not fear death himself can inflict it, but a prince need not fear much on this account, as such actions are extremely rare. He must only guard against committing any grave injury to any one he makes use of, or has about him for his service, like Antoninus had done, having caused the death with contumely of the brother of that centurion, and also threatened him every day, although he still retained him in his bodyguard, which was a foolish and dangerous thing to do, as the fact proved. But let us come to Commodus, who might easily have kept the empire, having succeeded to it by heredity, being the son of Marcus, and it would have sufficed for him to follow in the steps of his father to have satisfied both the people and the soldiers. But being of a cruel and bestial disposition, in order to be able to exercise his rapacity on the people, he sought to amuse the soldiers and render them licentious; on the other hand, by not maintaining his dignity, by often descending into the theatre to fight with gladiators and committing other contemptible actions, little worthy of the imperial dignity, he became despicable in the eyes of the soldiers, and being hated on the one hand and despised on the other, he was conspired against and killed. There remains to be described the character of Maximinus. He was an extremely warlike man, and as the armies were annoyed with the effeminacy of Alexander, which we have already spoken of, he was after the death of the latter elected emperor. He did not enjoy it for long, as two things made him hated and despised: the one his base origin, as he had been a shepherd in Thrace, which was generally known and caused great disdain on all sides; the other, because he had at the commencement of his rule deferred going to Rome to take possession of the Imperial seat, and had obtained a reputation for great cruelty, having through his prefects in Rome and

other parts of the empire committed many acts of
cruelty. The whole world being thus moved by
indignation for the baseness of his blood, and also by
the hatred caused by fear of his ferocity, he was
conspired against first by Africa and afterwards by
the senate and all the people of Rome and Italy. His
own army also joined them, for besieging Aquileia
and finding it difficult to take, they became enraged
at his cruelty, and seeing that he had so many
enemies, they feared him less and put him to death. I
will not speak of Heliogabalus, of Macrinus, or
Julian, who being entirely contemptible were
immediately suppressed, but I will come to the
conclusion of this discourse by saying that the
princes of our time have less difficulty than these of
being obliged to satisfy in an extraordinary degree
their soldiers in their states; for although they must
have a certain consideration for them, yet it is soon
settled, for none of these princes have armies that are
inextricably bound up with the administration of the
government and the rule of their provinces as were
the armies of the Roman empire; and therefore if it
was then necessary to satisfy the soldiers rather than
the people, it was because the soldiers could do more
than the people; now, it is more necessary to all
princes, except the Turk and the Soldan, to satisfy the
people than the soldiers, for the people can do more
than the soldiers. I except the Turk, because he
always keeps about him twelve thousand infantry
and fifteen thousand cavalry, on which depend the
security and strength of his kingdom; and it is
necessary for him to postpone every other
consideration of the people to keep them friendly. It
is the same with the kingdom of the Soldan, which

being entirely in the hands of the soldiers, he is bound to keep their friendship regardless of the people. And it is to be noted that this state of the Soldan is different from that of all other princes, being similar to the Christian pontificate, which cannot be called either a hereditary kingdom or a new one, for the sons of the dead prince are not his heirs, but he who is elected to that position by those who have authority. And as this order is ancient it cannot be called a new kingdom, there being none of these difficulties which exist in new ones; as although the prince is new, the rules of that state are old and arranged to receive him as if he were their hereditary lord. But returning to our matter, I say that whoever studies the preceding argument will see that either hatred or contempt were the causes of the ruin of the emperors named, and will also observe how it came about that, some of them acting in one way and some in another, in both ways there were some who had a fortunate and others an unfortunate ending. As Pertinax and Alexander were both new rulers, it was useless and injurious for them to try and imitate Marcus, who was a hereditary prince; and similarly with Caracalla, Commodus, and Maximinus it was pernicious for them to imitate Severus, as they had not sufficient ability to follow in his footsteps. Thus a new prince cannot imitate the actions of Marcus, in his dominions, nor is it necessary for him to imitate those of Severus; but he must take from Severus those portions that are necessary to found his state, and from Marcus those that are useful and glorious for conserving a state that is already established and secure.

XX. WHETHER FORTRESSES AND OTHER THINGS WHICH PRINCES OFTEN MAKE ARE USEFUL OR INJURIOUS

Some princes, in order to securely hold their possessions, have disarmed their subjects, some others have kept their subject lands divided into parts, others have fomented enmities against themselves, others have endeavoured to win over those whom they suspected at the commencement of their rule: some have constructed fortresses, others have ruined and destroyed them. And although one cannot pronounce a definite judgment as to these things without going into the particulars of the state to which such a deliberation is to be applied, still I will speak in such a broad way as the matter will permit of.

A new prince has never been known to disarm his subjects, on the contrary, when he has found them disarmed he has always armed them, for by arming them these arms become your own, those that you suspected become faithful and those that were faithful remain so, and from being merely subjects become your partisans. And since all the subjects cannot be armed, when you benefit those that you arm, you can deal more safely with the others; and this different treatment that they notice renders your men more obliged to you, the others will excuse you, judging that those have necessarily greater merit who have greater danger and heavier duties. But when you disarm them, you commence to offend them and show that you distrust them either through cowardice or lack of confidence, and both of these opinions generate hatred against you. And as you cannot remain unarmed, you are obliged to resort to a mercenary militia, of which we have already stated the value; and even if it were good it cannot be sufficient in number to defend you against powerful enemies and suspected subjects. But, as I have said, a new prince in a new dominion always has his subjects armed. History is full of such examples. But when a prince acquires a new state as an addition to his old one, then it is necessary to disarm that state, except those who in acquiring it have sided with you; and even these one must, when time and opportunity serve, render weak and effeminate, and arrange things so that all the arms of the new state are in the hands of your own soldiers who in your old state live near you.

Our forefathers and those who were esteemed wise used to say that it was necessary to hold Pistoia by means of factious and Pisa with fortresses, and for this purpose they fomented differences among their subjects in some town in order to possess it more easily. This, in those days when Italy was fairly divided, was doubtless well done, out does not seem to me to be a good precept for the present time, for I do not believe that the divisions thus created ever do any good; on the contrary it is certain that when the enemy approaches the cities thus divided will be at once lost, for the weaker faction will always side with the enemy and the other will not be able to stand. The Venetians, actuated, I believe, by the aforesaid motives, cherished the Guelf and Ghibelline factions in the cities subject to them, and although they never allowed them to come to bloodshed, they yet encouraged these differences among them, so that the citizens, being occupied in their own quarrels, might not act against them. This, however, did not avail them anything, as was seen when, after the defeat of Vaila, a part of those subjects immediately took courage and took from them the whole state. Such methods, besides, argue weakness in a prince, for in a strong government such dissensions will never be permitted. They are profitable only in time of peace, as by means of them it is easy to manage one's subjects, but when it comes to war, the fallacy of such a policy is at once shown. Without doubt princes become great when they overcome difficulties and opposition, and therefore fortune, especially when it wants to render a new prince great, who has greater need of gaining a great reputation than a hereditary prince, raises up enemies and compels him to undertake wars against them, so that he may have cause to overcome them, and thus raise himself higher by means of that ladder which his enemies have brought him. There are many who think therefore that a wise prince ought, when he has the chance, to foment astutely some enmity, so that by suppressing it he will augment his greatness. Princes, and especially new ones, have found more faith and more usefulness in those men, whom at the beginning of their power they regarded with suspicion, than in those they at first confided in. Pandolfo Petrucci, Prince of Siena, governed his state more by those whom he suspected than by others. But of this we cannot speak at large, as it varies according to the subject; I will merely say that these men who at the beginning of a new government were enemies, if they are of a kind to need support to maintain their position, can be very easily gained by the prince, and they are the more compelled to serve him faithfully as they know they must by their deeds cancel the bad opinion previously held of them, and thus the prince will always derive greater help from them than from those who, serving him with greater security, neglect his interest? And as the matter requires it, I will not omit to remind a prince who has newly taken a state with the secret help of its inhabitants, that he must consider well the motives that have induced those who have favoured him to do so, and if it is not natural affection for him, but only because they were not contented with the state as it was, he will have great trouble and difficulty in maintaining their friendship, because it will be impossible for him to content them. And on well examining the cause of this in the examples drawn from ancient and modern times it will be seen that it is much easier to gain the friendship, of those men who were contented with the previous condition and were therefore at first enemies, than that of those who not being contented, became his friends and helped him to occupy it. It has been the custom of princes in order to be able to hold securely their state, to erect fortresses, as a bridle and bit to those who have designs against them, and in order to have a secure refuge against a sudden assault. I approve this method, because it was anciently used. Nevertheless, Messer Niccolo Vitelli has been seen in our own time to destroy two fortresses in Città di Castello in order to keep that state. Guid' Ubaldo, Duke of Urbino, on returning to his dominions from which he had been driven by Cesare Borgia, razed to their foundations all the fortresses of that province, and considered that without them it would be more difficult for him to lose again the state. The Bentivogli, in returning to

Bologna, used similar measures. Therefore fortresses may or may not be useful according to the times; if they do good in one way, they do harm in another.

The question may be discussed thus: a prince who fears his own people more than foreigners ought to build fortresses, but he who has greater fear of foreigners than of his own people ought to do without them. The castle of Milan built by Francesco Sforza has given and will give more trouble to the house of Sforza than any other disorder in that state. Therefore the best fortress is to be found in the love of the people, for although you may have fortresses they will not save you if you are hated by the people. When once the people have taken arms against you, there will never be lacking foreigners to assist them. In our times we do not see that they have profited any ruler, except the Countess of Forli on the death of her consort Count Girolamo, for she was thus enabled to escape the popular rising and await help from Milan and recover the state; the circumstances being then such that no foreigner could assist the people. But afterwards they were of little use to her when Cesare Borgia attacked her and the people being hostile to her allied themselves with the foreigner. So that then and before it would have been safer for her not to be hated by the people than to have the fortresses. Having considered these things I would therefore praise the one who erects fortresses and the one who does not, and would blame any one who, trusting in them, thinks little of being hated by his people.

XXI. HOW A PRINCE MUST ACT IN ORDER TO GAIN REPUTATION

Nothing causes a prince to be so much esteemed as great enterprises and setting a rare example. We have in our own day Ferdinand, King of Aragon, at present King of Spain. He may almost be termed a new prince, because from a weak king he has become for fame and glory the first king in Christendom, and if you regard his actions you will find them all very great and some of them extraordinary. At the beginning of his reign he assailed Granada, and that enterprise was the foundation of his state. At first he did it leisurely and without fear of being interfered with; he kept the minds of the barons of Castile occupied in this enterprise, so that thinking only of that war they did not think of making innovations, and he thus acquired reputation and power over them without their being aware of it. He was able with the money of the Church and the people to maintain his armies, and by that long war lay the foundations of his military power, which afterwards has made him famous. Besides this, to be able to undertake greater enterprises, and always under the pretext of religion, he had recourse to a pious cruelty, driving out the Moors from his kingdom and despoiling them. No more admirable or rare example can be found. He also attacked under the same pretext Africa, undertook his Italian enterprise, and has lately attacked France; so that he has continually contrived great things, which have kept his subjects' minds uncertain and astonished, and occupied in watching their result.

And these actions have arisen one out of the

other, so that they have left no time for men to settle down and act against him. It is also very profitable for a prince to give some rare examples of himself in the internal administration, like those related of Messer Bernabò of Milan, when it happens that some one does something extraordinary, either good or evil, in civil life, and to take a means of rewarding or punishing him which will be much talked about. And above all a prince must endeavour in every action to obtain fame for being great and excellent. A prince is further esteemed when he is a true friend or a true enemy, when, that is, he declares himself without reserve in favour of some one against another.

This policy is always more useful than remaining neutral. For if two neighbouring powers come to blows, they are either such that if one wins, you will have to fear the victor, or else not. In either of these two cases it will be better for you to declare yourself openly and make war, because in the first case if you do not declare yourself, you will fall a prey to the victor, to the pleasure and satisfaction of the one who has been defeated, and you will have no reason nor anything to defend you and nobody to receive you. For, whoever wins will not desire friends whom he suspects and who do not help him when in trouble, and whoever loses will not receive you as you did not take up arms to assist his cause. Antiochus went to Greece, being sent by the Ætoli to expel the Romans. He sent orators to the Achæi who were friends of the Romans to encourage them to remain neutral, on the other hand the Romans persuaded them to take up arms on their side. The matter was brought before the council of the Achæi for deliberation, where the ambassador of Antiochus sought to persuade them to remain neutral, to which the Roman ambassador replied: "As to what is said that it is best and most useful for your state not to meddle in our war, nothing is further from the truth; for if you do not meddle in it you will become, without any favour or any reputation, the prize of the victor." And it will always happen that the one who is not your friend will want you to remain neutral, and the one who is your friend will require you to declare yourself by taking arms. Irresolute princes, to avoid present dangers, usually follow the way of neutrality and are mostly ruined by it. But when the prince declares himself frankly in favour of one side, if the one to whom you adhere conquers, even if he is powerful and you remain at his discretion, he is under an obligation to you and friendship has been established, and men are never so dishonest as to oppress you with such ingratitude.

Moreover, victories are never so prosperous that the victor does not need to have some scruples, especially as to justice. But if he to whom you adhere loses, you are sheltered by him, and so long as he can, he will assist you; you become the companion of a fortune which may rise again. In the second case, when those who fight are such that you have nothing to fear from the victor, it is still more prudent on your part to adhere to one; for you go to the ruin of one with the help of him who ought to save him if he were wise, and if he conquers he rests at your discretion, and it is impossible that he should not conquer with your help. And here it should be noted that a prince ought never to make common cause with one more powerful than himself to injure another, unless necessity forces him to it, as before said; for if he wins you rest at his discretion, and princes must avoid as much as possible being at the discretion of others. The Venetians united with France against the Duke of Milan, although they could have avoided that union, and from it resulted their own ruin. But when one cannot avoid it, as happened to the Florentines when the pope and Spain went with their armies to attack Lombardy, then the prince ought to join for the above reasons. Let no state believe that it can follow a secure policy, rather let it think that all are doubtful. This is found in the nature of things, that one never tries to avoid one difficulty without running into another, but prudence consists in being able to know the nature of the difficulties, and taking the least harmful as good. A prince must also show himself a lover of merit, and honour those who excel in every art. Moreover he must encourage his citizens to follow their callings quietly, whether in commerce, or agriculture, or any other trade that men follow, so that this one shall not refrain from improving his possessions through fear that they may be taken from him, and that one from starting a trade for fear of taxes; but he should offer rewards to whoever does these things, and to whoever seeks in any way to improve his city or state. Besides this, he ought, at convenient seasons of the year, to keep the people occupied with festivals and spectacles; and as every city is divided either into trades or into classes, he ought to pay attention to all these things, mingle with them from time to time, and give them an example of his humanity and magnificence, always holding firm, however, the majesty of his dignity, which must never be allowed to fan in anything whatever.

XXII. OF THE SECRETARIES OF PRINCES

The choice of a prince's ministers is a matter of no little importance; they are either good or not according to the prudence of the prince. The first impression that one gets of a ruler and of his brains is from seeing the men that he has about him. When they are competent and faithful one can always consider him wise, as he has been able to recognise their ability and keep them faithful. But when they are the reverse, one can always form an unfavourable opinion of him, because the first mistake that he makes is in making this choice. There was nobody who knew Messer Antonio da Venafro as the minister of Pandolfo Petrucci, Prince of Siena, who did not consider Pandolfo to be a very prudent man, having him for his minister. There are three different kinds of brains, the one understands things unassisted, the other understands things when shown by others, the third understands neither alone nor with the explanations of others. The first kind is most excellent, the second also excellent, but the third useless. It is therefore evident that if Pandolfo was not of the first kind, he was at any rate of the second. For every time that one has the judgment to know the good and evil that any one does or says, even if he has no invention, yet he recognises the bad and good works or his minister and corrects the one and supports the other; and the minister cannot hope to deceive him and therefore remains good. For a prince to be able to know a minister there is this method which never fails. When you see the minister think more of himself than of you, and in all his actions seek his own profit, such a man will never be a good minister, and you can never rely on him; for whoever has in hand the state of another must never think of himself but of the prince, and not call to mind anything but what relates to him. And, on the other hand, the prince, in order to retain his fidelity ought to think of his minister, honouring and enriching him, doing him kindnesses, and conferring on him honours and giving him responsible tasks, so that the great honours and riches bestowed on him cause him not to desire other honours and riches, and the tasks he has to fulfil make him fearful of changes, knowing that he could not execute them without the prince. When princes and their ministers stand in this relation to each other, they can rely the one upon the other; when it is otherwise, the end is always injurious either for one or the other of them.

XXIII. HOW FLATTERERS MUST BE SHUNNED

I must not omit an important subject, and a mistake which princes can with difficulty avoid, if they are not very prudent, or if they do not make a good choice. And this is with regard to flatterers, of which courts are full, because men take such pleasure in their own things and deceive themselves about them that they can with difficulty guard against this plague; and by wishing to guard against it they run the risk of becoming contemptible. Because there is no other way of guarding one's self against flattery than by letting men understand that they will not offend you by speaking the truth; but when every one can tell you the truth, you lose their respect. A prudent prince must therefore take a third course, by choosing in his state wise men, and giving these alone full liberty to speak the truth to him, but only of those things that he asks and of nothing else; but he must ask them about everything and hear their opinion, and afterwards deliberate by himself in his own way, and in these councils and with each of these men comport himself so that every one may see that the more freely he speaks, the more he will be acceptable. Outside these he should listen to no one, go about the matter deliberately, and be determined in his decisions. Whoever acts otherwise either acts precipitately through flattery or else changes often through the variety of opinions, from which it happens that he is little esteemed. I will give a modern instance of this. Pre' Luca, a follower of Maximilian, the present emperor, speaking of his majesty said that he never took counsel with anybody, and yet that he never did anything as he wished; this arose from his following the contrary method to the aforesaid. As the emperor is a secret man he does not communicate his designs to any one or take any one's advice, but as on putting them into effect they begin to be known and discovered, they begin to be opposed by those he has about him, and he is easily diverted from his purpose. Hence it comes to pass that what he does one day he undoes the next, no one ever understands what he wishes or intends to do, and no reliance is to be placed on his deliberations. A prince, therefore, ought always to take counsel, but only when he wishes, not when others wish; on the contrary he ought to discourage absolutely attempts to advise him unless he asks it, but he ought to be a great asker, and a patient hearer of the truth about those things which he has inquired of; indeed, if he finds that any one has scruples in telling him the truth he should be angry. And since some think that a prince who gains the reputation of being prudent is so considered, not by his nature but by the good councillors he has about him, they are undoubtedly deceived. It is an infallible rule that a prince who is not wise himself cannot be well advised, unless by chance he left himself entirely in the hands of one man who ruled him in everything, and happened to be a very prudent man. In this case he may doubtless be well governed, but it would not last long, for that governor would in a short time deprive him of the state; but by taking counsel with many, a prince who is not wise will never have united councils and will not be able to unite them for himself. The councillors will all think of their own interests, and he will be unable either to correct or to understand them. And it cannot be otherwise, for men will always be false to you unless they are compelled by necessity to be true.

Therefore it must be concluded that wise counsels, from whoever they come, must necessarily be due to the prudence of the prince, and not the prudence of the prince to the good counsels received.

XXIV. WHY THE PRINCES OF ITALY HAVE LOST THEIR STATES

The before-mentioned things, if prudently observed, make a new prince seem ancient, and render him at once more secure and firmer in the state than if he had been established there of old. For a new prince is much more observed in his actions than a hereditary one, and when these are recognised as virtuous, he gains men more and they are more bound to him than if he were of the ancient blood. For men are much more taken by present than by past things, and when they find themselves well off in the present, they enjoy it and seek nothing more; on the contrary, they will do all they can to defend him, so long as the prince is not in other things wanting to himself. And thus he will have the double glory of having founded a new realm and adorned it and fortified it with good laws, good arms, good friends and good examples; as he will have double shame who is born a prince and through want of prudence has lost it.

And if one considers those rulers who have lost their position in Italy in our days, such as the King of Naples, the Duke of Milan and others, one will find in them first a common defect as to their arms, for the reasons discussed at length, then we observe that some of them either had the people hostile to them, or that if the people were friendly they were not able to make sure of the nobility, for without these defects, states are not lost that have enough strength to be able to keep an army in the field. Philip of Macedon, not the father of Alexander the Great, but the one who was conquered by Titus Quinteus, did not possess a great state compared to the greatness of Rome and Greece which assailed him, but being a military man and one who knew how to divert the people and make sure of the great, he was able to sustain the war against them for many years; and if at length he lost his power over several cities, he was still able to keep his kingdom. Therefore, those of our princes who had held their possessions for many years must not accuse fortune for having lost them, but rather their own negligence; for having never in quiet times considered that things might change (as it is a common fault of men not to reckon on storms, in fair weather) when adverse times came, they only thought of fleeing from them, instead of defending themselves; and hoped that the people, enraged by the insolence of the conquerors, would recall them. This measure, when others are wanting, is good; but it is very bad to have neglected the other remedies for that one, for nobody would desire to fall because he believed that he would then find some one to pick him up. This may or may not take place, and if it does, it is not with safety to you, as that defence is known to be cowardly and not to be depended on; and only those defences are good, certain and durable, which depend only on yourself and your own ability.

XXV. HOW MUCH FORTUNE CAN DO IN HUMAN AFFAIRS AND HOW IT MAY BE OPPOSED

It is not unknown to me how many have been and are of opinion that worldly events are so governed by fortune and by God, that men cannot by their prudence change them, and that on the contrary there is no remedy whatever, and for this they may judge it to be useless to toil much about them, but let things be ruled by chance. This opinion has been more believed in in our day, from the great changes that have been seen, and are daily seen, beyond every human conjecture.

When I think about them at times, I am partly inclined to share this opinion. Nevertheless, that our freewill may not be altogether extinguished, I think it may be true that fortune is the ruler of half our actions, but that she allows the other half or a little less to be governed by us. I would compare her to an impetuous river that, when turbulent, inundates the plains, ruins trees and buildings, removes earth from this side and places it on the other; every one flies before it, and everything yields to its fury without being able to oppose it; and yet though it is of such a kind, still when it is quiet, men can make provision against it by dams and banks, so that when it rises it will either go into a canal or its rush will not be so wild and dangerous. It happens similarly with fortune, which shows her power where no measures have been taken to resist her, and turns her fury where she knows that no dams or barriers have been made to hold her. And if you regard Italy, which has been the seat of these changes, and who has given the impulse to them, you will see her to be a country without dams or barriers of any kind. If she had been protected by proper measures, like Germany, Spain, and France, this inundation would not have caused the great changes that it has, or would not have happened at all. This must suffice as regards opposition to fortune in general. But limiting myself more to particular cases, I would point out how one sees a certain prince to-day fortunate and to-morrow ruined, without seeing that he has changed in character or otherwise. I believe this arises in the first place from the causes that we have already discussed at length; that is to say, because the prince who bases himself entirely on fortune is ruined when fortune varies. I also believe that he is happy whose mode of proceeding accords with the needs of the times, and similarly he is unfortunate whose mode of proceeding is opposed to the times. For one sees that men in those things which lead them to the aim that each one has in view, namely, glory and riches, proceed in various ways; one with circumspection, another with impetuosity, one by violence, another by cunning, one with patience, another with the reverse; and each by these diverse ways may arrive at his aim. One sees also two cautious men, one of whom succeeds in his designs, and the other not, and in the same way two men succeed equally by different methods, one being cautious, the other impetuous, which arises only from the nature of the times, which does or does not conform to their method of proceeding. From this results, as I have said, that two men, acting differently, attain the same effect, and of two others acting in the same way, one arrives at his good and not the other. From this depend also the changes in fortune, for if it happens that time and circumstances are favourable to one who acts with caution and prudence he will be successful, but if time and circumstances change he will be ruined, because he does not change his mode of proceeding. No man is found able to adapt himself to this, either because he cannot deviate from that to which his nature disposes him, or else because having always prospered by walking in one path, he cannot persuade himself that it is well to leave it; and therefore the cautious man, when it is time to act suddenly, does not know how to do so and is consequently ruined; for if one could change one's nature with time and circumstances, fortune would never change. Pope Julius II. acted impetuously in everything he did and found the times and conditions so in conformity with that mode of proceeding, that he always obtained a good result. Consider the first war that he made against Bologna while Messer Giovanni Bentivogli was still living. The Venetians were not pleased with it, the King of Spain and likewise France had objections to this enterprise, notwithstanding which with his fierce and impetuous disposition he engaged personally in the expedition. This move caused both Spain and the Venetians to halt and hesitate, the latter through fear, the former through the desire to regain the entire kingdom of Naples. On the other hand, he engaged with him the King of France, because seeing him make this move and desiring his friendship in order to put down the Venetians, that king judged that he could not refuse him his troops without manifest injury. Thus Julius by his impetuous move achieved what no other pontiff with the utmost human prudence would have succeeded in doing, because, if he had waited till all arrangements had been made and everything settled before leaving Rome, as any other pontiff would have done, it would never have taken place. For the king of France would have found a thousand excuses, and the others would have inspired him with a thousand fears. I will omit his other actions, which were all of this kind and which all succeeded well, and the shortness of his life did not suffer him to experience the contrary, for had times succeeded in which it was necessary to act with caution, his ruin would have resulted, for he would never have deviated from these methods to which his nature disposed him. I conclude then that fortune varying and men remaining fixed in their ways, they are successful so long as these ways conform to each other, but when they are opposed to each other then they are unsuccessful. I certainly think that it is better to be impetuous than cautious, for fortune is a woman, and it is necessary, if you wish to master her, to conquer her by force; and it can be seen that she lets herself be overcome by these rather than by those who proceed coldly. And therefore, like a woman, she is a friend to the young, because they are less cautious, fiercer, and master her with greater audacity.

XXVI. EXHORTATION TO LIBERATE ITALY FROM THE BARBARIANS

Having now considered all the things we have spoken of, and thought within myself whether at present the time was not propitious in Italy for a new prince, and if there was not a state of things which offered an opportunity to a prudent and capable man to introduce a new system that would do honour to himself and good to the mass of the people, it seems to me that so many things concur to favour a new ruler that I do not know of any time more fitting for such an enterprise. And if, as I said, it was necessary in order that the power of Moses should be displayed that the people of Israel should be slaves in Egypt, and to give scope for the greatness and courage of Cyrus that the Persians should be oppressed by the Medes, and to illustrate the pre-eminence of Theseus that the Athenians should be dispersed, so at the present time, in order that the might of an Italian genius might be recognised, it was necessary that

Italy should be reduced to her present condition, and that she should be more enslaved than the Hebrews, more oppressed than the Persians, and more scattered than the Athenians; without a head, without order, beaten, despoiled, lacerated, and overrun, and that she should have suffered ruin of every kind. And although before now a spirit has been shown by some which gave hope that he might be appointed by God for her redemption, yet at the highest summit of his career he was thrown aside by fortune, so that now, almost lifeless, she awaits one who may heal her wounds and put a stop to the rapine and pillaging of Lombardy, to the rapacity and extortion in the kingdom and in Tuscany, and cure her of those sores which have long been festering. Behold how she prays God to send some one to redeem her from this barbarous cruelty and insolence. Behold her ready and willing to follow any standard if only there be some one to raise it. There is nothing now she can hope for but that your illustrious house may place itself at the head of this redemption, being by its power and fortune so exalted, and being favoured by God and the Church, whose leadership it now occupies. Nor will this be very difficult to you, if you call to mind the actions and lives of the men I have named. And although those men were rare and marvellous, they were none the less men, and had each of them less occasion than the present, for their enterprise was not juster than this, nor easier, nor was God more their friend than He is yours. Here is a just cause; for that war is just which is necessary; and those arms are merciful where no hope exists save in them. Here is the greatest willingness, nor can there be great difficulty where there is great willingness, provided that the measures are adopted of those whom I have set before you as examples. Besides this, unexampled wonders have been seen here performed by God, the sea has been opened, a cloud has shown you the road, the rock has given forth water, manna has rained, and everything has contributed to your greatness, the remainder must be done by you. God will not do everything, in order not to deprive us of freewill and the portion of the glory that falls to our lot It is no marvel that none of the before-mentioned Italians have done that which it is to be hoped your illustrious house may do; and if in so many revolutions in Italy and so many warlike operations, it always seems as if the military capacity were extinct, this is because the ancient methods were not good, and no one has arisen who knew how to discover new ones. Nothing does so much honour to a newly-risen man than the new laws and measures which he introduces. These things, when they are well based and have greatness in them, render him revered and admired, and there is not lacking scope in Italy for the introduction of every kind. Here there is great virtue in the members, if it were not wanting in the heads. Look how in duels and in councils of a few the Italians are superior in strength, dexterity, and intelligence. But when it comes to armies they make a poor show; which proceeds entirely from the weakness of the leaders, for those that know are not obedient, and every one thinks that he knows, there being hitherto nobody who has raised himself so high both by valour and fortune as to make the others yield. Hence it comes about that in all this time, in all the wars waged during the last twenty years, whenever there has been an army entirely Italian it has always been a failure, as witness first Taro, then Alexandria, Capua, Genoa, Vaila, Bologna, and Mestri. If your illustrious house, therefore, wishes to follow those great men who redeemed their countries, it is before all things necessary, as the true foundation of every undertaking, to provide yourself with your own forces, for you cannot have more faithful, or truer and better soldiers. And although each one of them may be good, they will together become better when they see themselves commanded by their prince, and honoured and supported by him. It is therefore necessary to prepare such forces in order to be able with Italian prowess to defend the country from foreigners. And although both the Swiss and Spanish infantry are deemed terrible, none the less they each have their defects, so that a third order might not only oppose them, but be confident of overcoming them. For the Spaniards cannot sustain the attack of cavalry, and the Swiss have to fear infantry which meets them with resolution equal to their own. From which it has resulted, as will be seen by experience, that the Spaniards cannot sustain the attack of French cavalry, and the Swiss are overthrown by Spanish infantry. And although a complete example of the latter has not been seen, yet an instance was furnished in the battle of Ravenna, where the Spanish infantry attacked the German battalions, which observe the same order as the Swiss. The Spaniards, through their bodily agility and aided by their bucklers, had entered between and under their pikes and were in a position to attack them safely without the Germans being able to defend themselves; and if the cavalry had not charged them they would have utterly destroyed them. Knowing therefore the defects of both these kinds of infantry, a third kind can be created which can resist cavalry and need not fear infantry, and this will be done not by the creation of armies but by a change of system. And these are the things which, when newly introduced, give reputation and grandeur to a new prince. This opportunity must not, therefore, be allowed to pass, for letting Italy at length see her liberator. I cannot express the love with which he would be received in all those provinces which have suffered under these foreign invasions, with what thirst for vengeance, with what steadfast faith, with what love, with what grateful tears. What doors would be closed against him? What people would refuse him obedience? What envy could oppose him? What Italian would rebel against him? This barbarous domination stinks in the nostrils of every one. May your illustrious house therefore assume this task with that courage and those hopes which are inspired by a just cause, so that under its banner our fatherland may be raised up, and under its auspices be verified that saying of Petrarch:

> Valour against fell wrath
> Will take up arms; and be the
>   combat quickly sped I
> For, sure, the ancient worth,
> That in Italians stirs the heart, is
>   not yet dead.